EARLY WILLS
1746–1765
LUNENBURG COUNTY
VIRGINIA

COMPILED
BY
KATHERINE B. ELLIOTT
SOUTH HILL
VIRGINIA

Please direct all correspondence and orders to:

www.southernhistoricalpress.com
or
SOUTHERN HISTORICAL PRESS, Inc.
PO BOX 1267
375 West Broad Street
Greenville, SC 29601
southernhistoricalpress@gmail.com

ISBN #0-89308-377-1

Printed in the United States of America

PREFACE

The Act dividing Brunswick County and creating the County of Lunenburg was passed by the House of Burgesses on 26 March 1745/46.

This Act provided "That from and immediately after the first day of May next, the said County of Brunswick be divided", and provided further "That after the first day of May, a court for the said County of Lunenburg be constantly held by the justices thereof, on the first Monday in every month".

A Commission of the Peace for organizing the new county was directed to John Hall, William Howard, Matthew Talbot, Lewis Delony, John Phelps, William Hill, John Caldwell, Cornelius Cargill, Abraham Cook, Hugh Lawson, Thomas Lanier, and William Caldwell, Gentlemen.

The meeting to organize the county government was held on the 5th day of May 1746, but the exact place at which this meeting was held is not of record. The June Court was held at the home of Thomas Bouldin (now Charlotte County), and the July Court was held at Burwell's Quarter on Butcher's Creek (now Mecklenburg County).

Lunenburg County (as established 5 May 1746) covered a vast area, and this area was eventually cut into eleven counties. That part of Lunenburg County south of the Staunton and Blackwater Rivers was cut off in 1752 to form the County of Halifax.

The area north of these rivers, and west of the present County of Charlotte (which then included a part of the present County of Appomattox), was cut off in 1753 to form the County of Bedford. After that date, Lunenburg County consisted of the area now Charlotte, Lunenburg and Mecklenburg Counties until 1765. Charlotte and Mecklenburg Counties were cut from Lunenburg County in 1765.

With the exception of an adjustment in the county line, between Charlotte and Lunenburg Counties in 1778, the area of Lunenburg County has been the same since 1765. A small section of Charlotte County was cut off in 1778, and added to Lunenburg County.

Cumberland Parish was established as the first parish of the new county. The area of this parish was reduced when Halifax and Bedford Counties were cut from Lunenburg. Cumberland Parish was cut into Cornwall and Cumberland in 1757. Cornwall Parish became Charlotte County in 1765. The parish was divided again in 1761 into Cumberland and St. James, and the latter parish became Mecklenburg County in 1765.

Clayton Torrence, in "Virginia Wills and Administrations - 1632-1800", published in 1930, stated that these records of Lunenburg County were complete. But it now appears that this statement has to be questioned. There seem to be quite a number of records of wills and administrations now missing.

The earliest records of wills and administrations for Lunenburg County are bound in the back of Deed Book 1. The will books then begin with Will Book No. 1, and are numbered consecutively. The first of these records in Deed Book 1, is dated 7 July 1746, and the last entry is dated 2 April 1751.

While the first entry in Will Book 1 is dated 1 Dec. 1746, this is the only entry for the year 1746. There is only one entry recorded for the year 1747. The records are then in chronological order to 1 May 1759, but on page 254 there is found an entry dated 6 March 1748/49. Subsequent dates of recording are mixed. The first entry in Will Book 2 gives date of recording as 3 Aug. 1762, but this is followed by an entry recorded 5 Aug. 1760. The third entry is listed as being recorded 1 June 1762, and is followed by an entry recorded 5 May 1761.

This seems to indicate that the early wills and administrations were not recorded in books but compiled at a later date from loose papers then extant. An examination of the Court Order Books discloses orders without corresponding entries in the will books. The compilers can only conclude that many records were never recorded and are now lost.

The Court Order Books are intact, and with one exception are numbered consecutively. Each book has a separate index. Between Order Book 2 and 3, there are two volumes containing more than a thousand pages which are numbered 2½-A and 2½-B. There are no indexes for these two volumes. Chronologically these two volumes follow Order Book 2.

Lunenburg County does not have any Guardian Books, and records of the appointments of guardians are found in the order books. The accounts of guardianships are recorded also in the order books.

Because so many references to early estates appear in the order books without corresponding entry in the will books, the compilers have included entries from the order books as an annotation to this volume. These notes are believed to be of value in placing family relationship not disclosed in the will books.

After the establishment of Cornwall Parish, there appear in the order books many orders of the court directed to the church wardens of Cornwall Parish to bind out children.

These orders do not give the names of the parents, or indicate whether the parents were living or dead. But from the number of such orders, it seems that one or both of the parents were dead though not indicated in the orders. These orders have not been included in the annotations given.

There appears in the order books occasional entries of orders to church wardens to bind out children "for reasons known to the Court", but without further explanation. This qualification, however, does not appear in many of the orders.

The records in this volume cover the period 1746 to 1766. The area of Lunenburg County was so vast that after 1752-1753 many of the names appearing in this volume have to be searched for in the records of Halifax and Bedford Counties.

Herbert A. Elliott

CONTENTS

LUNENBURG COUNTY WILLS

ABSTRACTS

SMITH, Edmond — Deed Book 1, Page 35

Inventory and appraisal of the goods and chattels of Edmond Smith, late of Brunswick County, deceased, made 24 June 1746 by Christ^r Gist, Adam Beird (?), Tim^o Connor and An^d Smith, administrator - value 50 pounds 13 shillings 3 pence.
Returned by Anne Smith, administratrix

Recorded 7 July 1746

GREEN, Henry — Deed Book 1, Page 477

NAMES: Wife - Elizabeth Green
Sons - Eldest son John - plantation where he (John) now lives plus 157 acres more.
- Second son Henry - 157 acres to include the plantation where Abigail Green, relict of my brother John Green, now lives.
- Third son Stephen - 157 acres to include an old field whereon John Russell formerly lived.
- Fourth son Frederick - 157 acres to be laid off at the lower end of the tract I now hold.

Lend to wife Elizabeth, during her widowhood, remaining 157 acres including plantation where I now live.

In case my wife die or marry, said tract is to go to youngest son Richard.

Personal estate to remain in hands of my wife and, at her death or marriage, to be divided among all children excluding sons John and Henry and daughter Dorcas who are sufficiently provided for.

Executors: Brother-in-law Richard Griffin and son John Green

Witnesses: Edward (E) Sizemore — /s/ Henry (H) Green
William (X) Jackson
Thos Greenwood

Will dated 15 Oct. 1748 — Recorded *

* Date not recorded but before 5 June 1749

HOWARD, Francis — Deed Book 1, Page 479

NAMES: Wife - Dianna Howard
Bequest to wife of negroes for her natural life.
Children - Eldest daughter Elizabeth one negro.
Daughter Elenor one negro.
Son William one negro. - Son Francis one negro.
Daughter Dianna one negro. - Daughter Hannah one negro.

Daughter Dianna one negro. - Daughter Hannah one negro.
To Cousin Mary Howard 15 pounds, feather bed when she marries or comes to lawful age.
All rest of my personal estate to be divided among my wife and all of my aforesaid children when the eldest shall come to age or marry.

Executors: Wife Dianna and brother William Howard
Witnesses: John Hyde
Henry Delony
William Sandifer

/s/ Francis (X) Howard

Will dated 6 Feb. 1748 — Recorded 5 June 1749

McCLARY, William — Deed Book 1, Page 481

Inventory and appraisal of the personal estate of William McClary, deceased, made 15 April 1749 by Wm Irby, Thos. Finney and John Philpot - value 11 pounds 19 shillings 7 pence.
Returned by Ephraim Hill, administrator

Recorded 5 June 1749

LEE, David — Deed Book 1, Page 481

Inventory and appraisal of the personal estate of David Lee made by Robt Wood, David Logan and James Warkup - value 56 pounds 3 shillings.
Returned by Eliz^a^ Lee, administrator

Recorded 5 June 1749

VAUGHAN, James — Deed Book 1, Page 484

NAMES: Wife - not named and deceased.
Son - Reuben Vaughan 400 acres on Pine Creek at head of Antnor (?) Creek, slaves and furniture.
Son - Stephen Vaughan 400 acres adjoining Mrs. Brodnax, a negro wench (her first child to go to James Vaughan his brother), a bed and furniture.
Son - James Vaughan the plantation (his) father now lives on.
Daughter - Lura Vaughan one side saddle.
Remainder of my estate to be equally divided among my children.

Executor: (son) Reuben Vaughan
Witnesses:
William (W) Andros (Andrews)
Richard (K) Andros (Andrews)

/s/ James Vaughan

Will dated 20 July 1740 — Recorded 3 July 1750

SEYMOOR, Thomas — Deed Book 1, Page 484

NAMES: Wife - Sarah Seymoor
To George Seymoor 100 acres of land where I now live.
To William Seymoor 100 acres of land.
To John Sparrow 100 acres of land at the place where he made his beginning.
To wife Sary Seymoor all of my movable estate to live on during her natural life.

Executors: Wife and John Sparrow

Witnesses: James Wood
Ephraim Hill /s/ Thomas (X) Seymoor
John (ᴵR) Philpot

Will dated 22 Nov. 1748 Recorded 4 July 1749

DAVID, Adlar Deed Book 1, Page 486

NAMES: Wife - not named and deceased.
Daughter - Ann Tindman David - slaves
Daughter - Elenor David - slaves - one to be given her after the death of Koziah Chambers.
Friend Andrew Wade - land on Difficult Creek which I bought of William Irby.

Executor: Friend Samuel Harris

Witnesses: Andrew Wade /s/ David Adlar
John Cook
Henry Wade

Will dated 15 May 1749 Recorded 5 July 1749

MICHAUX, Abraham Deed Book 1, Page 487

Inventory and appraisal of the goods and chattels of Abraham Michaux, deceased, taken at his late dwelling in Lunenburg County 9 Nov. 1749 by John Nance, Tandy Walker and Sylvanus Walker - value 30 pounds 0 shillings 1 pence.

Recorded 4 July 1749

McDAVID, James Deed Book 1, Page 488

NAMES: Wife - mentioned in will but not by name.
Son - Eldest son John McDavid 100 acres of land where he now lives.
Son-in-law - James McLaughlin 100 acres of land where he is now improving next to the land of son John.
Sons - George and Patrick McDavid the tract of land where I now live containing 291 acres and likewise 50 acres of above tract of land of which John and James are entitled.
Personal estate to stand and be handled by the executors for wife and children not of age.

Executors: Thomas Doughorty and son George to be executors and guardians for children under age.

Witnesses: /s/ James McDavid
Thos Doughorty
John McDavid
Will dated 10 March 1748/49 Recorded 3 Oct. 1749

ECHOLS, Abraham Deed Book 1, Page 489

NAMES: Wife - Sarah Echols
Bequest to wife - chattèls and plantation where he lives for her natural life.
Son - Eldest son Isaac Echols to get plantation at death of wife Sarah Echols,
Son - Youngest son Joshua Echols given land next to plantation given to wife.
Son - Joseph Echols land on Stinking River.
Daughter - Sarah Echols (one-half of) land on Staunton River against the Long Island.
Daughter - Rebekah Echols (one-half of) land on Staunton River against the Long Island.
Daughter - Elizabeth Echols my entry for land on Stinking River.
Brother - Joseph Echols land and mill on Childreys Creek.
Brother-in-law - Benjamin Hubbard, my wife's brother my land on Bentleys Fork of Childreys Creek.
Brother-in-law - Mentions Edward Hubbard my wife's brother.
Executors: Wife Sarah Echols, Joseph Echols and Richard Echols.
Witnesses: Joseph Collins /s/ Abraham (X) Echols
George (X) Marshbank
Will dated 2 April 1749 Recorded 3 Oct. 1749

JONES, Robert Deed Book 1, Page 491

NAMES: Wife - not mentioned and evidently deceased.
Son - Brerton Jones - My gold seal ring he already having his portion. (Brereton)
Son - Robert Jones
Son - William Jones
Bequest - Land where I now live to be equally divided between sons Robert and William Jones.
Son - Thomas Jones
But if I fail to get the land (entry) on the Little Horsepen Creek, then son Thomas to have one-third of the land where I now live to begin at the place where he now has a cornfield.
Son - Samuel Jones

Son - Charles Jones
Sons Robert, William and Thomas Jones are to purchase for my sons Samuel and Charles Jones 200 acres of good plantable land and the money is to be repaid from the sale of lands which I have in the Northern Neck to be sold by my executors.

But if the 900 acre survey on Little Horsepen Creek comes through, then this land to be divided equally between sons Thomas, Samuel and Charles Jones, and no 200 acres is to be bought.

Five daughters - Betty Girth, Mary Foot, Margrit Jones, Nanny Jones and Looanna Jones to be paid 100 pounds each.

Negroes and personal estate to be divided among my five sons Robert Jones, William Jones, Thomas Jones, Samuel Jones and Charles Jones.

Executors: Sons Robert, William and Thomas Jones and their brother Brereton Jones.

Witnesses: J° Perrin
Robarrah (R) Perrin /s/ R Jones
William Perrin

Will dated 9 Sept. 1748 Recorded 4 Oct. 1749

WILDS, Luke (Luke Wiles) Deed Book 1, Page 493

NAMES: Wife - Margaret Wiles
Bequest - to wife Margaret plantation for her natural life.
Land on Deep Creek in Gougland (Goochland ?) County to be sold by my executors to pay my debts.
The land I now live on (on the lower side of the Roanoke River) to be surveyed and equally divided amongst my four sons.
Son - Eldest son Robert Wilds - first choice.
Son - Thomas Wilds - second choice.
Son - Stephen Wilds - third choice
Son - Luke Wilds - last choice.
Two daughters - not named - to be given a cow each when they are of age.
After death of my wife, estate to be divided among all of my children.

Executors: Wife Margaret and son Robert Wilds.

Witnesses: Josiah Seat
David H. Embry /s/ Luke (Luke) Wilds
Thomas Wilds

Will dated 31 May 1749 Recorded 2 Jan. 1749/50

Note: Margaret Wilds, widow, qualified as executrix on the estate of Luke Wilds with Tandy Walker and Thomas Dupree her securities.

DUGLAS, Alex[r] (Alexander Douglas) Deed Book 1, Page 494

Inventory of the estate of Alex[r] Duglas, deceased, taken 5 Sept. 1749 by Richard Witton, administrator, and appraised by Mr. John Twitty, John Doak and Joseph Green, value 9 pounds 13 shillings - returned to Court.

Recorded 2 Jan. 1749/50

HOWARD, Francis Deed Book 1, Page 495

Appraisal of the estate of Francis Howard, deceased, made by Thos. Stovall, John Speed and William Abbitt - value 360 pounds 13 shillings 1½ pence - returned to Court by Dianah (E) Farrar and William Howard (executors).

Recorded 2 Jan. 1749/50

BILBO, John Peter Deed Book 1, Page 496

NAMES: Wife - Elizabeth Bilbo
Son - James Bilbo 300 acres of land (being part) of tract I now live on to be laid off on the upper side of the creek.
Son - Joseph Bilbo 300 acres on lower side of the creek.
Son - John Bilbo 300 acres adjoining the above tract.
Son - Peter Bilbo 300 acres adjoining the last mentioned tract.
Son - William Bilbo the ramainder of my tract, the whole tract by estimation contains 1626 acres.
Bequests - Two cows to be given each son.
Isaac Dutoy - Tract of land in Cumberland County in consideration of the sum of 12 pounds already paid to me.
Wife Elizabeth - She is to possess the land bequeathed to (son) Joseph which includes the plantation for her natural life.
My wife Elizabeth to enjoy the remainder of my estate for life, and at her death to be divided among my children James, John, Peter, William, Joseph, Mary, Elizabeth and Sarah Bilbo.

Executors: Wife Elizabeth Bilbo and Joseph Chandler
Witnesses: Joseph Greer
John Goure (Gorre)
Joseph Chandler /s/ John Peter Bilbo
Isaac Dutoy

Will dated 15 Nov. 1750 Recorded 2 April 1751

CALDWELL, John Deed Book 1, Page 498

John Caldwell of Cub Creek in Virginia.
Estate to be inventoried and left in the power of my

executors for the use and support of my children that shall be under age at my decease.

NAMES: Wife - not named in will and evidently deceased.

Son - Eldest son William Caldwell 400 acres of land where he now lives, 12 pounds 10 shillings in cash and (my) Great Bible.

Son - John Caldwell 400 acres known by the name Flag Spring, and my executor is to make deed to him when he thinks proper, also 100 acres where mill now stands with mill and all improvements. Mill to be left rented or sold for the use of (son) John as the discretion of my executor.

Son - James Caldwell 500 acres where I now live.

Son - David Caldwell 500 acres of land on the east side of Cub Creek, being part of a tract of 1080 acres by estimation, and likewise 100 acres of land on west side of Cub Creek, being part of the tract aforesaid, to begin at the mouth of Louse Creek.

Son - Robert Caldwell 600 acres on west side of Cub Creek, a part of it being in the aforesaid tract of 1080 acres, and the remainder being 300 acres adjoining the aforesaid land lying on Walkers Branch.

My executor is empowered to sell and title the remainder of the aforesaid 1080 acres lying above the mouth of Walkers Branch adjoining John Short for the use and support of my children that shall be under age at my death.

I leave to my three sons John, Robert and James Caldwell all of my horses, geldings, mares and colts to be equally divided between them at the discretion of my executor.

Executor: David Caldwell, and he is to be guardian of any of my children under age at my death.

Witnesses: Wm Rogers
George Moore /s/ John Caldwell
John McNess

Will dated 26 Nov. 1748 Recorded 3 April 1751

SULLIVANT, John Deed Book 1, Page 500

A true and perfect inventory of the estate of John Sullivant, deceased, made on 18 March 1750 by John Gwinn, Henry Isbell and William (X) Maddox - value 58 pounds 14 shillings.

Recorded 2 April 1751

CALDWELL, William Deed Book 1, Page 501

William Caldwell being weak in body but of sound mind.

NAMES: Wife - Joan Caldwell
Bequest - My wife Joan to have a full third of my personal estate after my debts are paid - to be sold or (divided) at the discretion of my executors.
Son - Eldest son Thomas Caldwell
Son - John Caldwell
Bequest - To two eldest sons Thomas and John Caldwell one tract of land containing 177 acres lying on Sandy Creek.
I order that my children be bound out by my executors as they think proper.
As soon as my wife shall think proper to leave the plantation where I now live, I order it to be sold by my executors for the use of my three youngest children (not named), and the remainder of my personal estate to be laid out for the use of my children as my executors may think proper.
Executors: James Caldwell and Thomas Doughorty
Witnesses: Wm Caldwell, Junr.
David Caldwell /s/ William Caldwell
John McNess
Will dated 22 Dec. 1750 Recorded 2 April 1751

SMITH, William Deed Book 1, Page 502

William Smith of Cumberland Parish, Lunenburg County, being sick and weak in body, etc.
NAMES: Wife - Elizabeth Smith
Bequest - My wife Elizabeth to have all of my lands, plantation and moveable goods for her natural life provided she don't marry or alter her way of living, but if she does, she shall have due (her) one third of my land, plantation and personal property only during her natural life.
Son - John Smith - to have maintenance out of said estate until he is of full age, then he shall be possessed of two-thirds of my land and personal property.
At the death of my wife, all that has been given to her shall go to my son John Smith.
Executor: Wife Elizabeth Smith
Witnesses: Hugh Lawson
Ben (illegible) /s/ William (X) Smith
Isabel (X) White
Will dated 16 May 1750 Recorded 2 April 1751

BRACKENRIDGE, Jean (Breckenridge ?) Will Book 1, Page 1

NAMES: Daughter - Lettice Brackenridge

Bequest - To daughter Lettice my bed, furniture, pots, pans and all other property.
Executor: Mr. John Twitty
Witnesses: John Wall /s/ Jean (θ) Brackenridge
Adam Brackenridge
Will dated 3 Aug. 1746 Recorded 1 Dec. 1746

CALDWELL, Thomas Will Book 1, Page 1

Inventory and appraisal of the estate of Thomas Caldwell, deceased, made by Israel Pirkens, John Stewart and Andrew Cunningham - value 65 pounds 5 shillings. Returned to Court by William Caldwell, Gent., administrator.

Recorded 7 March 1747

HAYNES, William Will Book 1, Page 3

Inventory and appraisal of the estate of William Haynes, deceased, made 26 Sept. 1747 by James Anderson, William (illegible) and Mattox Mayes - value 8 pounds 4 shillings.

Recorded 7 March 1747/48

BALLEW, William Will Book 1, Page 3

Inventory and appraisal of the estate of William Ballew taken 9 July 1747 by Tho Satterwhite, John Wilkins and William Tabor - value 17 pounds 14 shillings 11½ pence.

Recorded 6 June 1748

BALLEW, William Will Book 1, Page 4

Account of sales of the personal estate of William Ballew, deceased, - 20 pounds 14 shillings 10 pence - returned to Court by George Currie, administrator.

Recorded 6 June 1748

COOK, Abraham Will Book 1, Page 6

Inventory of the personal estate of Abraham Cook, deceased, returned to Court by Sarah (Z) Cook.

Recorded 4 July 1748

COOK, Abraham Will Book 1, Page 7

Will of Abraham Cook of Cumberland Parish, Lunenburg County.
NAMES: Wife - Sarah Cook
Bequest - Wife Sarah all of my estate for her natural life.
Daughter - Sarah Cook - To have negro Hannah after death of my wife.

Daughter Sarah Cook to have a bed, also, but if she dies without heirs then her part to go to my son Benjamin Cook and his heirs.
Daughter - Barbary Hester - 1 shilling.
Daughter - Frances Hester - 1 shilling.
Son - James Cook - 1 shilling.
Son - Benjamin Cook the land and plantation where I now live to him and his heirs forever.
Son - Charles Cook my land on Sandy Creek for use of his heirs.
Balance of my estate to go to my sons Benjamin and Charles Cook.

Executors: Wife Sarah and son Benjamin Cook
Witnesses: Richard Palmer
Thomas Satterwhite /s/ Abraham Cook
John (Illegible))

Will dated 2 April 1748 Recorded 4 July 1748

RAMBOE, Christopher Will Book 1, Page 8

NAMES: Thomas Pinson, Elinor Pinson, John Pinson, Sarah Ann Pinson (Connection not stated)
Aaron Pinson, Senr. (Connection not stated)
Bequests: To Thomas Pinson, Elinor Pinson, John Pinson and Sarah Ann Pinson horses cattle and other personal property.
To Aaron Pinson hogs and other estate.

Executor: William Hancock
Witnesses: William Hancock /s/ Christopher (C) Ramboe
Aaron (A) Pinson, Junr.

Will dated 7 Nov. 1747 Recorded 1 Aug. 1748

Note: William Hancock refused to qualify and Aaron Pinson qualified as administrator with the will annexed.

LEE, David Will Book 1, Page 11

David Lee of the County of Brunswick *

NAMES; Wife - Elizabeth Lee
Bequest to wife - One-third of personal estate after debts are paid, horse and saddle, use of the plantation where I now live for her widowhood.
Son - David Lee - Tract of land beginning at the mouth of the first branch above Clay Ford on Wards Fork ... to the line of Andrew Kennedy ... and to Caldwells Mill path ... one gray mare.
Sons - John Lee and Clement Lee - All of the remainder of the tract of land I bought of Matthew Talbott (except land to son David and what shall be hereafter mentioned) to be divided.

Son Clement to have that part of the land that includes the plantation where I now live ... it being a part of the tract of 1800 acres of land I bought of Talbott.
Son-in-law - John Morris a tract of land on Wards Fork, being part of the aforesaid 1800 acres, lying on the lower side of the mouth of the first branch above the Clay Ford.
Son-in-law - Andrew Kennedy a tract of land (200 acres) being a part of the aforesaid 1800 acres.
Son-in-law - Abel Lee - bequest 5 pounds.
Son - Joshua Lee - bequest 10 shillings.

Executors: Wife Elizabeth Lee and friend Thomas Jones.
Witnesses: Matthew Talbott, William (M) Owen and John Roakby.

Will dated 10 March 1743/44 Recorded 3 Oct. 1748

Note: Elizabeth Lee qualified as executrix.

* Will dated 10 March 1744 before Lunenburg County was cut from Brunswick County in 1746. The will of David Lee was recorded twice - on pages 9-10 and 11-12.

KENNEDY, Andrew Will Book 1, Page 13

Inventory of the estate of Andrew Kennedy, deceased, taken by David Caldwell, David Logan and Robert Woods 15 Oct. 1748 - value not given - returned to Court by Elizabeth C. Kennedy, administratrix.

Recorded 6 Feb. 1749

Will Book 1, Page 14

An account of the sales of the personal estate of Andrew Kennedy, deceased, made 29 October 1748.

Recorded 6 Feb. 1749

DOUGLAS, Alexander Will Book 1, Page 15

An account rendered by Richard Witton, administrator of the estate of Alexander Douglas, deceased, of sale at Public Venue in October last at Lunenburg Court.

Recorded 2 Jan. 1749

SEYMORE, Thomas Will Book 1, Page 15

A true inventory of the estate of Thomas Seymore, deceased, made by William Irby, William Gent and Robert Wynne - value 19 pounds 3 shillings 10 pence.

Recorded 3 July 1750

WYLES, Luke (Luke Wiles) Will Book 1, Page 16

In obedience to an Order of Court 9 January to us - John Wilkins, Thos Satterwhite and Richd Palmer - we made an inventory and appraisal of the estate of Luke Wyles, deceased, - no total value given.

Recorded 3 July 1750

WAKUP, James * Will Book 1, Page 17

NAMES: Wife - Ellonir Wakup
Daughters - Martha and Easter Wakup
Estate to be appraised except for iron gray mare and saddle (now known by the name of my daughter Martha's) these to be hers.
All other personal property to be sold and to be equally divided between my wife Ellonir and my two daughters Martha and Easter Wakey (sic).
Land to be divided into two long tracts - Martha to have tract next to David Logan - wife to have plantation tract where I live, and then to go to daughter Easter.
Executors: Friends John Stewart and Wm Caldwell
Witnesses: David Logan, James Murphy, George (H) Harrel
Will dated 23 Sept. 1750 Recorded 2 Oct. 1750

* Will signed "James Warkup". Executors named qualified

SULLIVANT, John Will Book 1, Page 19

NAMES: Wife - mentioned in will but not by name.
Daughters - Sarah Melone, Elizabeth Sullivant, Hannah Sullivant, Mary Sullivant.
Bequest - 800 acres of land lying on the north side of Twittys Creek ... being land between Twittys Creek and Randolphs Road ... to be divided equally between my four daughters.
Sons - James Sullivant, Manoah Sullivant, John Sullivant.
The remaining part of my land, being 2400 acres or thereabouts, to be equally divided amongst them.
My youngest son John to have the plantation where I now live, and my eldest son James to have his choice of the rest.
Rest of my estate to be used for the support of my wife and children until they come of age or marry. As they come of age or marry, I desire their part to be given to them.
Executors: Brother(s) Charles Sullivant and Owen Sullivant
Witnesses: Thomas Bouldin and John Gwin
Will dated 3 August 1750 Recorded 2 Oct. 1750

LANGLEY, John — Will Book 1, Page 21

Inventory and appraisal of the estate of John Langley, deceased, made by Thomas Stevens, Jacob Mitchell and Isaac Mitchell - value 22 pounds 4 shillings 6 pence - returned to Court by Margaret Langley.

Recorded 2 Oct. 1750

JONES, Robert — Will Book 1, Page 22

An inventory of the estate of Robert Jones, deceased, returned to Court by Robert Jones, William Jones and Thos Jones, executors - no value given.

Recorded 2 Oct. 1750

VAUGHAN, James — Will Book 1, Page 23

An inventory and appraisement of the estate of James Vaughan, deceased, made 25 Sept. 1750 by William Hagood James Arnoll and John Watson - value 152 pounds 16 shillings 7 pence - returned to Court.

Recorded 2 Oct. 1750

TATE, Patrick — Will Book 1, Page 24

A true inventory of the estate of Patrick Tate, deceased, made 29 Sept. 1750 by William Irby, John Hanna and John Legrand - value 15 pounds 2 shillings -. returned to Court.

Recorded 2 Oct. 1750

GLASS, Joshua — Will Book 1, Page 25

Inventory and appraisal of the goods and chattels of Joshua Glass, deceased, made 16 July 1750 by Thomas Eastland, Thomas Lanier and Isaac Mitchell - value 17 pounds 9 shillings 3 pence - returned to Court.

Recorded 2 Oct. 1750

Will Book 1, Page 25

An account rendered for the estate of Joshua Glass, deceased, by James Knott, administrator, approved by James Mitchell and Julius Nichols (commissioners) 3 April 1751 (sic).

Recorded 2 Oct. 1750

CALDWELL, Thomas — Will Book 1, Page 26

An account current of the estate of Thomas Caldwell, deceased, (many names including the widow, Jane Caldwell, mentioned), approved by Thomas Bouldin and Abra. Martin, (commissioners).

Recorded 2 Oct. 1750

CORNELIUS, Joseph — Will Book 1, Page 28

An account of the estate of Joseph Cornelius, deceased, adjusted 3 August 1750 by Abra. Martin and Thomas Bouldin (commissioners).

Recorded 3 Oct. 1750

DAY, Thomas — Will Book 1, Page 29

An account current of the estate of Thomas Day returned to Court. By Order of the Court, we have settled and adjusted the said account 3 August 1750.
Signed: Abra. Martin and Thomas Bouldin (commissioners)

Recorded 3 Oct. 1750

MICHAUX, Abraham — Will Book 1, Page 30

Nuncupative Will of Abraham Michaux, Amelia County - 31 December 1747.

"This day Peleg Farguson came before me, one of the Justices, and said that on the 28 November 1747 he was at the dwelling house of Abraham Michaux and in his company, and he, Abraham Michaux, being very sick and likely to dye, desired the said Farguson to write a few lines for meaning his will and testament. His desire was that William Turker should have what he was possessed with (except) only one black heifer which he gave to his sister Susanna Quinn, but if William Turker died without heirs, then John Michaux, Junr., and Abraham Michaux, his brother, sons of John Michaux should come in for his estate.
The he asked Farguson to fetch his pocket book and read him his old will, and he did, and he said the things (that) John Michaux had he was not possessed with himself, meaning his moulds, so he asked Farguson to tear off his signature, and that he (Abraham Michaux) died before he could finish the writing and the above writing is the last will and testament of Abraham Michaux, deceased!" /s/ Peleg Farguson

Certified by Charles Irby

Presented at Court for probate 2 August 1748

Court decided that the will was a good (or valid) one, and ordered probate of same. Lydall Bacon, Gent., with John Bacon and Lewis Delony his securities, entered into and acknowledged bond (as administrator).

Recorded 3 Oct. 1750

GRIFFIN, William — Will Book 1, Page 31

NAMES: Wife - mentioned in will but not by name.
Son - William Griffin
Daughter - Elizabeth Griffin

Bequest - Lend to wife plantation with 300 acres pertaining thereto during her widowhood and then to son William Griffin. Gives to wife personal property and stock.

Bequests: To son William personal property.
To daughter Elizabeth one feather bed when she becomes age 18 years.
To Henry Green, son of John Green, 100 acres of land on Buffalo Creek to be laid off at upper end of my land.
To Ralph Griffen, son of Richard Griffin, 100 acres of land adjoining Henry Green on the lower side.

Household goods not before given to be equally divided among my son and daughter.

Guns and one horse to be sold for support of my family.

Executors: Ralf (sic) Griffin, William Woodward and my wife (name not stated).

Witnesses: William Tarkson
William Sizemore
Charles Smith

/s/ William (Ø) Griffin

Will dated 17 Oct. 1750 — Recorded 2 April 1751

VAUGHAN, James — Will Book 1, Page 32

An additional appraisement of a part of the estate of James Vaughan, deceased, made by James Arnoll and John Watson, appraisers - no valuation given - including a negro man to Reuben Vaughan, a negro man to Steven Vaughan, a negro man to James Vaughan, being legacies to the children of James Vaughan, deceased.

Recorded 2 April 1751

HATCHER, Benjamin — Will Book 1, Page 33

NAMES: Wife - none mentioned in will

Bequests: To nephew Benjamin Hatcher, son of my brother Jeremiah, a negro when he arrives at age 21. If he dies then to Edward Goode Hatcher, son of my brother Jeremiah.
To nephew Edward Goode Hatcher a negro when he arrives at age 21. If he dies then to nephew Benjamin Hatcher.
If both should die, then both negroes to nephew Robert Hatcher, son of my brother Jeremiah.
To niece Mary Hatcher, daughter of my brother Jeremiah, 10 pounds to be raised from the labor of the above (mentioned) negroes and paid when she is of age.

To brother Jeremiah Hatcher all of the residue and remainder of my estate both real and personal.

Executors: Brother Jeremiah and his wife Margrita Hatcher

Witnesses: Edward Goode /s/ Benjamin (X) Hatcher
William Mackendow

Will dated 27 June 1750 Recorded 3 April 1751

POWELL, Richard Will Book 1, Page 34

NAMES: Wife - Martha Powell
Son - John Powell - bequest one shilling.
To wife Martha Powell all of estate not mentioned for her widdwhood - if she doesn't marry, she may dispose of estate at her death - if she marries, then estate to descend to my (other ?) six children - Richard Powell, David Powell, Mary Powell, Martha Powell, Sary Powell and Judith Powell.

Executor: Wife Martha to be sole executor.

Witnesses: Sam[l] Harris
John (B) Bolding /s/ Rich[d] (RP) Powell
Andrew Wade

Will dated 15 May 1749 Recorded 3 April 1751

RODGERS, William Will Book 1, Page 35

NAMES: Wife - Margaret Rodgers
Children - mentioned but not by name
Do appoint and ordain David Caldwell, Thomas Rodgers and my wife Margaret Rodgers to divide and title my land among my children at their discretion ... and to sell any part they judge necessary for the support of my family during their noneage ?.

Executor: None specifically named.

Witnesses: John McNess
James Anderson /s/ W Rodgers
Robert Mitchell
Henry Pattillo

Will dated 15 Oct. 1750 Recorded 3 April 1751

LAWSON, Mary Will Book 1, Page 36

NAMES: Son - Francis Lawson - bequest 20 shillings
To his daughter Mary 20 shillings
To John Boyd and his wife Margrit 5 shillings and the one-half of my body ?.
To David Sheerer and wife Ann 5 shillings.
To John Lawson a coalt (colt) called Ball.
To Alexander Irwin and his wife 10 shillings.
To his daughter (not named) 10 shillings.
The (other) half of my body I leave to my dau-

ghter Mary Lawson.
The remainder of my worldly goods I leave to my three sons, John Lawson, William Lawson and David Lawson, to be equally divided between them.
I leave to Isobel Boyd one five year old horse and saddle.

Executors: Sons John and William Lawson
Witnesses: John Dalharte
Mary Evan(s) ? /s/ Mary (M) Lawson
David Graham

Will dated 15 Oct. 1749 Recorded 2 April 1751

GLASS, Joshua Will Book 1, Page 37

1750 - An account of the estate of Joshua Glass, deceased, returned to Court by James Knott (administrator) approved and ordered recorded.

Recorded 5 April 1751

WILLINGHAM, John Will Book 1, Page 38

NAMES: Wife - Mary Willingham
Son - Thomas Willingham - one shilling sterling.
Son - John Willingham - one shilling sterling.
(I have already given them - my two sons - what I desired for them)
Daughter - Christian Willingham - one slave.
Son - Gerrald Willingham - negro boy, household goods, land and plantation where I now live and 90 acres of land adjoining said plantation.
I desire that my wife shall have possession of my land for widowhood or life.
The residue of my estate to my wife for life and then to be equally divided between my two daughters Amey and Betty Willingham.

Executor: Wife Mary Willingham
Witnesses: Geo. Walton /s/ John (X) Willingham
Tsth Degraffenreid
George Martin

Will dated 2 Feb. 1750 Recorded 1 Oct. 1751

MAYS, William (William Mayes) Will Book 1, P. 39

NAMES: Wife - Mary Mayes
Son - William Mayes - the plantation he now lives on, and all of the land belonging on the upper side of Hat Creek being part of 400 acres. I also give to him the plantation I now live on on the Roanoak in Lunenburg.
Son - Mattox Mayes - one Indian slave
Son - Joseph Mayes - three Indian slaves

Daughter - Frances White for natural life the plantation where she now lives containing 120 acres, and all that part of the above tract that lies between Hat Creek and a branch known as the dividing line branch.
If my daughter and her husband leave, rent, destroy or sell any timber, the land to go to my grandson William Childrey. If she does comply with (my) conditions, then land to go to William Childrey at her death.

Bequest - Frances White given, also, an Indian slave, and at her death to my two grandsons Thomas and William Childrey.

To Thomas Childrey 150 acre tract of land on the east side of the dividing branch.

Wife Mary Mayes to have an Indian slave, and at her death to go to son Joseph Mayes.

Granddaughter - Mary Mattox Giles - an Indian slave, but if she dies without heirs slave to go to my son Mattox Mayes.

Daughter - Lucy Ellis - gives hogs.

Wife Mary Mayes to have balance of estate for her natural life, and after her decease to son Joseph Mayes.

Executors: Sons Mattox and Joseph Mayes
Witnesses: James Hunt
William (W) Faris /s/ Wm Mays
George Abney

Will dated 8 Nov. 1748 Recorded 1 Oct. 1751

STOKES, Elizabeth Will Book 1, Page 42

I Elizabeth Stokes formerly of Charles City County but now of Brunswick County. *
NAMES:
Son - Richard Stokes - one rug value 20 shillings and one sheet value 10 shillings.
Son - David Stokes - residue of my estate both real and personal.

Executor: Son David Stokes
Witnesses: Lyddall Bacon /s/ Eliz Stokes
John Bacon
Drury Allin

Will dated 27 April 1746 Recorded 1 Oct. 1751

* Will made before Lunenburg County was cut from Brunswick County.

TAIT, William (William Tate ?) Will Book 1, Page 43

NAMES: Wife - Sarah Tait

Son - James Tait - one shilling sterling
Daughter - Mary Jeter - one shilling sterling
Son - John Tait - one shilling sterling
Son - Thomas Tait - one shilling sterling
Son - Nathaniel Tait - one shilling sterling and one heifer
Daughter - Sarah Tait - one shilling sterling
Daughter - Lucy Tait - one shilling sterling
Wife - Sarah Tait - Plantation where I now live and after her death to my son William.
Sons - Nathaniel Tait, Samuel Tait and Jesse Tait my entry of land to be equally divided between them.
Daughter - Elizabeth Tait - 5 pounds money.
Rest of my personal estate to be equally divided between my sons Nathaniel, Samuel and Jesse and daughters Elizabeth and Sarah Tait after the death of my wife Sarah Tait.

Executor: Wife Sarah Tait
Witnesses: Matthew Tanner /s/ William Tait
Rebecca Hawkins
Will dated 2 April 1751 Recorded 2 Oct. 1751

EDWARDS, Thomas, Senr. Will Book 1, Page 44

NAMES: Wife - Martha Edwards
Son - Eldest son John Edwards - 5 pounds money
Sons - William Edwards, Thomas Edwards, James Edwards, Isham Edwards and Henry Edwards
Bequest: Land to be equally divided between my sons - William first share, Thomas next, Isham next, Henry next and James next share.
Daughter - Mary Edwards - 10 pounds on day of her marriage or at age 21.

Executors: Wife Martha and son William Edwards
Witnesses: John Bullock
Tho[s] Gresham /s/ Thomas (TE) Edwards
Mary (M) Garnes
Will dated 29 March 1751 Recorded 2 Oct. 1751

PATTERSON, Daniel Will Book 1, Page 46

NAMES: Wife - none named in will
Daughter - Catherin Patterson
Daughter - Ann Patterson
Bequest: To my two daughters, or either of them, coming over from Ireland, all of my personal estate.
If either of my daughters (do) not come over sea to enjoy same, then I give said personal estate to my executor William Lawson.
My executor is to make an equal division of the rest of my estate between him and his two brothers John and David Lawson.

Executor: William Lawson

Witnesses: Enoch Armitage
Alex[r] Irwin /s/ Daniel Petterson
Euphemie (T) Trapnell
James (illegible)

Will dated 12 Aug. 1751 Recorded 2 Oct, 1751

BROWN, William Will Book 1, Page 47

NAMES: Wife - none named in will
God daughter - Elizabeth Mobarly (daughter of Edward and Susanna Mobarly)
Bequest: To Elizabeth Mobarly my land and plantation where I now live and all land I am now possessed with.
To Giles Williams all my goods and chattels.
Executors: Edward Mobarly and Giles Williams
Witnesses: Clement Mobarly
Joseph Williams /s/ William Brown
John Williams

Will dated 15 Feb. 1750 Recorded 2 Oct. 1751

Note: Edward Mobarly qualified as executor with John Echols and Clement Mobarly his securities.

DOBYNS, William Will Book 1, Page 48

Inventory of the estate of William Dobyns, deceased, as it was appraised - value 164 pounds 9 shillings 3 pence - returned to Court by John Cox, administrator.

Tyree Glenn, Jesse Brown and Valentine Brown met at the plantation of William Dobyns, deceased, and appraised all that was brought before them in obedience to order of Court.

Recorded 2 Oct. 1751

RAGSDALE, Godfrey Will Book 1, Page 50

NAMES: Wife - none named in will
First I desire that my plantation in Amelia County be sold, and whereas one hundred pounds can be had for it, I bequeath it as follows:
To Peter Ragsdale, son of Jo[s] Ragsdale, 40 pounds.
To Brother Drury Ragsdale's children 20 pounds - that is Drury Ragsdale (Junr.) and Frances Ragsdale. The money to put to interest until they come of age or marry. If either should die the money to go to my brother Joseph Ragsdale.
To my brother * Richard Witton 20 pounds.
(* Brother-in-law)

To brother Joseph Ragsdale one negro.
Executor: Mr. Richard Witton
Witnesses: And^{w} Graham /s/ Godfrey (G) Ragsdale
Thos^{s} (T) Larnders
Will dated 26 April 1751 Recorded 3 Oct. 1751

EALIDGE, Francis Will Book 1, Page 51

NAMES: Wife - Mary Ealidge
Son - William Ealidge - all the land I am possessed of when I depart this life and personal property.
Daughter - Mary Ealidge - negro and furniture.
Daughter - Elizabeth Land - negro and stock. If the negro outlives Elizabeth Land, then the negro is to go to her eldest son Ealidge Land
All of the rest of my estate to my wife Mary Ealidge.
Executor: Wife Mary Ealidge
Witnesses: John G. Parnall /s/ Francis Ealidge
James E. Smith
Christopher Hudson
Will dated 20 Oct. 1750

Codicil dated 27 July 1751
Wife Mary Ealidge has permission to sell part or all of my lands to pay debts.
Recorded 3 Oct. 1751

Note: Mary Ealidge qualified as executrix with Richard Witton and Hampton Wade her securities.

Will Book 1, Page 53

Inventory and appraisal of the estate of Francis Ealidge made by John Speed, Christopher Hudson and Martin Fifer (Phifer) - value 209 pounds 12 shillings 11 pence - returned to Coutt by Mary Ealidge and order-to be recorded.
Recorded 7 Jan. 1752

TAIT, William Will Book 1, Page 54

Inventory and appraisal of the estate of William Tait, deceased, made by order of Court by Thomas Hawkins, John Clark and Fran^{s} Bressie - value 35 pounds 10 shillings - returned to Court by Sarah Tait - Ordered to be recorded.
Recorded 7 Jan. 1752

HATCHER, Benjamin — Will Book 1, Page 55

Inventory and appraisal of the estate of Benjamin Hatcher agreeable to the order of the Lunenburg County made by Edw. Goode, Nicholas Hobson and Wm Markadue - value 104 pounds 8 shillings - returned to Court 6 Jan. 1752 ordered recorded.

Recorded 7 Jan. 1752

BILBO, John Peter — Will Book 1, Page 55

Inventory and appraisal of the estate of John Peter Bilbo, deceased, made by Joseph Greer, Christopher Hudson and John Humphreys - value 138 pounds 18 shillings 3 pence - returned to Court by Elizabeth Bilbo.

Recorded 7 Jan. 1752

HOWARD, Captain William — Will Book 1, Page 56

Inventory and appraisal of the estate of Capt. William Howard by order of the Court made by William Sandefer, John Speed and Hutchins Burton - value 22 pounds 7 shillings 6 pence - returned to Court by Thomas Hawkins

Recorded 7 Jan. 1752

Will Book 1, Page 57

Further inventory and appraisal of the estate of William Howard made 1 July 1751 by William Sandefer, John Speed and Henry Delony - value 187 pounds 2 shillings 9 pence - returned to Court by Thomas Hawkins and ordered to be recorded.

Recorded 7 Jan. 1752

MORFIELD, John — Will Book 1, Page 59

Inventory and appraisal of the estate of John Morfield made by Charles Allen, Jonathon Ashworth and Samuel Ashworth - value 20 pounds 5 shillings - returned to Court.

Recorded 7 Jan. 1752

CUNNINGHAM, Thomas — Will Book 1, Page 59

Thomas Cunningham of Brunswick County *

NAMES: Wife - Darkus (Dorcas) Cunningham
Sons - Thomas and John Cunningham - Sons to divide small (personal) estate and moveables on plantation.
Daughter - Mary Cunningham - one horse.
Wife Darkus to live on plantation, or if she moves to have a reasonable support.

Executors: Friends John Caldwell and Willian Cunningham and to be overseers. Son Thomas to be my administrator
Witnesses: John Caldwell and William Cunningham

Codicil - 10 Sept. 1745
Before signing it is my will that my three children that are in Pennsylvania, having received their share, (be given) one shilling each - that is, James Cunningham, Ann Cunningham, alias Wilson and Margaret Cunningham, alias McCoy.
/s/ Thomas (I) Cunningham
Will dated 10 Sept. 1745 Recorded 7 April 1752

* Will made before Lunenburg County was cut off from Brunswick County.

WALKER, Juday * Will Book 1, Page 61

I desire that all real and personal property be sold at Public Dandue (sic) Vendue, and money to be divided among my seven sons and daughters, namely, Silvanus Walker, Tandy Walker, William Walker, Joel Walker, Lankford Walker, Ann Walker and Elizabeth Walker.
My sons to be of age at 20 years and receive their part, and my daughters to be of age at 18 years. They to receive their part at age 18 or on day of marriage.
Executors: Friends Ludwell Bacon, Sylvanus Walker and Thomas Dupree all of Lunenburg County.
Witnesses: Jas. Scott
Henry Hatcher /s/ Juday (X) Walker
Thos. Williamson

Codicil: I earnestly request that this last desire of mine may be fulfilled, that Henry Fowlkes take Tandy, Sylvanus Walker take William and Joel, Thomas Dupree take Lankford and Elizabeth and that Tyree Glenn take Ann.
Witnesses: Jas. Scott /s/ Juday (X) Walker
Henry Hatcher
Thos. Williamson
Dated 29 Feb. 1752 Recorded 7 April 1752

* Juday Walker, widow of Tandy Walker, deceased.

PATTERSON, Daniel Will Book 1, Page 63

Inventory and appraisal of the estate of Daniel Patterson, deceased, made by James Irwin, Evan Evans and William Douglas - value 26 pounds 3 shillings 2½ pence - returned by William Lawson, executor.
Made 6 Jan. 1751/52 Recorded 7 April 1752

BLANKS, Joseph — Will Book 1, Page 63

Inventory and appraisal of the estate of Joseph Blanks, deceased, made by Arthur Freeman, Phillemon Russell and Wm Saffold - value 102 pounds 12 shillings 6 pence.
Recorded 7 April 1752

BAKER, Samuel — Will Book 1, Page 64

A true and perfect inventory of the goods and chattels of Samuel Baker, deceased, taken at his late dwelling house in the County of Lunenburg this 15 April 1751 by John Bacon, William Jeter and John Hayes, returned to Court by Margritt Baker, administrator.
Recorded 7 April 1752

WILLINGHAM, John — Will Book 1, Page 65

Lunenburg Court 6 Dec. 1751
In obedience to the Order of Court the first day of October last, we the subscribers - Geo. Walton, Tscharner Degraffenreid and Thompson Staples - met at the plantation of John Willingham, deceased, and appraised said estate - value 191 pounds 15 shillings 6 pence. Returned to Court by Mary Willingham, executrix.
Recorded 7 April 1752

BROWN, William — Will Book 1, Page 67

Inventory taken 17 December 1751 of the estate of William Brown, deceased, by Thomas Pitman, John Mobley and Glidewell Orrill - value 11 pounds 6 shillings 6 pence - returned to Court by Giles Williams, admin.
Recorded 8 April 1752

BARRY, John — Will Book 1, Page 67

Inventory of the personal estate of John Barry, deceased, taken by Richard Leak, Reapps Jones and Saml Jones - no total given.
Recorded 8 April 1752

MICHAUX, Abraham — Will Book 1, Page 68

Account current of Lydall Bacon, executor of the estate of Abraham Michaux, ordered to be recorded.
Recorded 7 April 1752

BROWN, William — Will Book 1, Page 69

Account current of the estate of William Brown, deceased, returned by Giles Williams, executor.
Recorded 8 April 1752

WALKER, Tandy — Will Book 1, Page 70

Inventory and appraisal of the estate of Tandy Walker, deceased, made 21 Jan. 1752, by William Perry and Chas Allen, returned to Court. Recorded 8 April 1752

Will Book 1, Page 70

Appraisal made 21 Jan. 1752 by William Perry and Chas Alleh - value 186 pounds 12 shillings 3 pence. Further inventory of the estate of Tandy Walker, deceased, made 29 May 1752 by Wm Roberts, Chas Allen, William Perry and James Burton - value 135 pounds 16 shillings - returned to Court by Silvanus Walker (administrator), ordered recorded.

Recorded 2 June 1752

STOKES, Elizabeth — Will Book 1, Page 71

Inventory of the goods and chattels of Elizabeth Stokes deceased, taken 1 May 1752, by David Stokes, executor, returned to Court.

Recorded 5 May 1752

USSERY, John — Will Book 1, Page 72

Inventory and appraisal of the estate of John Ussery, deceased, made by Reeps Jones, William Rivers and Robert Moore - value 62 pounds 4 shillings 9 pence - returned to Court by Wm Ussery, administrator.

Recorded 5 May 1752

NOBLE, Robert — Will Book 1, Page 72

NAMES: Wife - not named in will and evidently deceased
Son - Joseph Noble - one shilling sterling.
Son - Robert Noble - all my lands and plantation on the southside of the Mehearing (sic) River at the mouth of Flat Rock Creek. If son Robert dies without heirs, all my lands and plantation to my grandson Joseph Noble, Junr.

Executor: Son Robert Noble

Witnesses: John Powell, John (O) Murfe, William Parker — /s/ Robbert (P) Nobbel

Will dated 1 Sept. 1750 — Recorded 7 June 1752

Note: Court says that executor Robert Noble is an infant under age of 20 years - administration with will annexed granted to Francis Wray.

BLANKS, Thomas — Will Book 1, Page 74

NAMES: Wife - mentioned in will but not by name. *
Son - Richard Blanks ... 107 acres of land, it being part of the tract that I now live on to be laid off at the lower end.
Son - William Blanks ... remainder of said tract of land.
Bequest: To loving wife ... horse and saddle.
To wife and two sons all of the residue of my estate to be equally divided.
To son Richard one entry of land containing 400 acres lying on Banister River.
To son William one entry of land containing 375 acres lying on Sandy Creek and one entry of land on Buffalo Creek.
Executors: Wife and son William Blanks
Witnesses: James Cocke
Aaron (A) Williams /s/ Tho. Blanks
Alex[r] (A) Strange

Will dated 26 March 1752 — Recorded 2 June 1752

* Hannah Blanks qualified as executrix on the estate.

SIMMONS, Charles — Will Book 1, Page 76

Inventory and appraisal of the goods and chattels of Charles Simmons, last of this County, deceased, made by Nicholas Haile, John Greer and James Standeford, - value 8 pounds 18 shillings 9 pence - returned to Court by John Talbot, administrator.

Recorded 2 June 1752

RAGSDALE, Godfrey — Will Book 1, Page 77

Appraisement of the estate of Godfrey Ragsdale, deceased, made 20 July 1751 by William White, Jos. Greer and Philip Poindexter - value 45 pounds 10 shillings - returned to Court by Richard Witton (executor).

Recorded 2 June 1752

CALDWELL, Henry — Will Book 1, Page 77

NAMES: Wife - none named in will
All debts to be paid.
Executors to relinquish all right and title to a certain tract of land on Cubb Creek in Lunenburg County, and to return the land to its former owners ... they refunding money I paid and to relinquish bonds.
Balance of my estate to be divided equally among my brother William Caldwell's five children ...

Thomas, John, Henry, Martha and Jean Caldwell.
Executors: James Caldwell, Senr., and Thomas Daughtery
Witnesses: W[m] Caldwell
David Caldwell /s/ Henry Caldwell
John Caldwell

Will dated 27 April 1752 Recorded 7 July 1752

Note: Thomas Daughtery qualified 7 July 1752.
Lunenburg Court 4 August 1752
James Caldwell, one of the executors appointed, relinquished his right to William Caldwell who qualified as executor.

WASKEY, James Will Book 1, Page 79

Inventory and appraisal of the estate of James Waskey, deceased, made by Richard Dudgeon, David Caldwell and John Logan - value 86 pounds 16 shillings 3 pence - returned to Court.

Recorded 4 Aug. 1752

SIMMONS, Charles Will Book 1, Page 81

Inventory and an account of sales of goods comprising the estate of Charles Simmons, deceased - value 9 pounds 14 shillings 1 pence - returned to Court by John Talbot, administrator.

Recorded 7 Nov. 1752

BILBO, John Peter Will Book 1, Page 82

An account current of the estate of John Peter Bilbo, deceased, returned by Eliz Winders, administratrix. Account approved by Robert Wooding and Philip Poindexter, commissioners.

Recorded 8 Nov. 1752

GWIN, David Will Book 1, Page 84

NAMES: Wife - mentioned will but not by name. Wife Mary named as one of the executors.
Grandson - John Gwin all my land and plantation where my son John Gwin (deceased ?) lived on the lower side of Ward's Fork. John Gwin (grandson) given 4 negroes, but if he dies without heirs all of above land and negroes to go to my son David Gwin.
Granddaughter Mary Glenn - Grandson John Qwin is to give his sister Mary Glenn a valuable piece of land.
Son - David Gwin all of the remainder of my land on the lower side of Ward's Fork and

my mill, mill land, negroes, money, household goods and books.

Son - George Gwin land and plantation where I now live, land adjoining on the upper side of Ward's Fork, negroes, money, etc.

Daughter - Jane Mattox money and a slave

Daughter - Druscilla Talbot money and a slave

" I desire that Mary Young, widow, may be found in bred (sic) corn during her natural life out of the corn got by my mill". (Connection not stated)

I give my wife liberty to make use of any part of my landed estate and negroes as she may think proper during her natural life.

Daughter - Sarah Gwin all of that land whereon the church standeth, Great Bible, money and negroes.

Executors: Son David and wife Mary Gwin
Witnesses: Clem[t] Read
Clem Read, Junr. /s/ David Gwin
Judith Showers

Will dated 20 Aug. 1752 Recorded 5 Dec. 1752

Notation: Mary Gwin, wife of David Gwin, deceased, qualified. David Gwin may do so later when he be of lawful age, if he should think proper.

GWIN, David Will Book 1, Page 87

Inventory and appraisal of the estate of David Gwin, deceased, made by Jos. Perrin, Charles Sullivant and Owen (O) Sullivant 30 December 1752, returned to Court by Mary (vc) Gwin, Ext. - value 402 pounds 9 shillings 6 pence.

Recorded 1 May 1753

BAKER, Samuel Will Book 1, Page 88

Account of sales of the estate of Samuel Baker, deceased. An inventory of the estate of Samuel Baker, deceased, as it was sold 5 Jan. 1853 and 3 Feb. 1853 - lists names, commodities and price - total 66 pounds 11 shillings 9 pence - returned to Court.

Recorded 6 Feb. 1853

Will Book 1, Page 90

3 Dec. 1752 - We have this day met at the plantation of Samuel Baker, deceased, and have settled and adjusted matters relating to the said estate, and do find a balance in favour of the said estate of 64 pounds 10 shilings. /s/ Lyddal Bacon and Geo. Walton

Recorded 6 Feb. 1753

GARRARD, Joseph — Will Book 1, Page 91

In obedience to an order of the Worshipful Court of Lunenburg County, dated 2 June 1752, on the motion of Hampton Wade, administrator of the estate of Joseph Garrard, deceased, we, the appraisers, do value the estate of the said decadent as follows: Inventory and appraisal at 46 pounds 5 shillings 3 pence.
Given under our hands 1 March 1753, /s/ Thos Winn, John Winn and Richard Stokes.

Recorded 1 March 1753

HOWARD, Francis — Will Book 1, Page 93

Account current of the estate of Francis Howard, deceased, approved 4 July 1753, by Philip Poindexter and Geo. Walton, comm.

Recorded 4 July 1753

FREEMAN, Arthur — Will Book 1, Page 94

NAMES: Wife - Agnes Freeman
Son - Hamblin Stokes Freeman my Spring Swamp land in Surry and all of the land on the south side of Kettlestick, after my father's decease, it is the land that Bershaba now lives on, to him and his heirs lawfully begotten forever.
Son - Henry Freeman the tract of land I now live on, excepting the child my wife Agnes now goes with (if it) should be a boy then to be divided equally between Henry Freeman and this boy as followeth: Begin at the mouth of the Spring branch at Flatrock (and) running up the branch to Bershabays Path thence a east corce (sic) to Kettlestick.
Son - Joel Freeman my tract of land lying in Surry and on the Nottoway River to him and his heirs forever.
Rest of my estate I lend for use of my wife during her life or widowhood.
Executor: Wife Agnes Freeman
Witnesses: Fillimon (R) Russell
John Calleham — /s/ Arthur Freeman
John Howell

Will dated 16 April 1753 — Recorded 3 July 1753

COCKE, James — Will Book 1, Page 96

NAMES: Wife - mentioned in will but not by name
Daughter - Martha Cocke - Bequest 500 pounds to be paid out of estate when she attain

to age of 18 years or marries.
Provided that the said Martha do acquit her right to a legacy left her by her grandfather James Powell Cocke as by his said will may more fully appear.

Daughter - Elizabeth Cocke - Bequest 500 pounds to be paid out of estate when she attain to age of 18 years or marries.

Son - James Cocke my tract of land called Malvern Hills containing 670 acres lying in County of Henrico, and another tract of land in the County of Cumberland containing 750 acres. Sixteen negroes now on the plantation of Malvern Hills, stock and household goods there. Five negroes now in Lunenburg County. I have given him (previously) three negroes which I have in Amelia County.

Soh - Chastain Cocke all of the land I have on the south side of the Staunton River in the County of Halifax - it being 2560 acres, and all the stock there. I gave him (previously) several negroes which are on the said land.

Son - Stephen Cocke my tract of land whereon I now dwell containing 300 acres, four negroes on said estate and what stock is on the plantation. I gave him several negroes which are in Amelia County.

I lend my wife my tract of land in Amelia County containing 2771 acres, all stock there and the 21 negroes who came with her for her natural life, and then to son Stephen Cocke, if he shall survive her. If not, to son James (but) if he does not then to son Chastain. If he dies, then to my daughters, but if no heirs survive, my wife to dispose of the 21 negroes as she sees fit.

Godson - James Dupuy 50 pounds to be paid by my executors when he reaches age 18.

If all my children die, all my estate except what I left to my wife to be equally between the three sons of Braizure Cocke.

Executors: My nephew John James Dupuy, his son Bartholomew Dupuy and his son-in-law John Trabue.

Witnesses: Hannah (X) Austin
Henry May
Ja[s] Scott
William Wassels

/s/ James Cocke

Will dated 30 April 1753 Recorded 3 July 1753

Notation under will of James Cocke. John James Dupuy, Bartholomew Dupuy and John James Trabue qualified on the estate with George Walton, Robert Wade, Stephen Mallet and Godfrey Jones their securities.

HAYES, Mark — Will Book 1, Page 100

NAMES: Wife - Ann Hayes
Children - Thomas Hayes, Mary Hayes, John Hayes
I desire that my just debts be paid.
I give remaining part of my moveable estate unto (my) well beloved wife ... towards the support of those children which I leave behind me in her care ... my lands are to be sold to best advantage by my wife (whom I also appoint sole executrix) and the money to be divided between my wife and those three children spoken of (namely) Thomas Haies, Mary Haies, John Haies.
Executor: My wife Ann Haies to be Executor and Trustee for children.
Witnesses: Rice Price
Thomas Price — /s/ Mark Haies
Robert Allen
Will dated 7 Dec. 1752 — Recorded 7 Aug. 1753

MOSS, William — Will Book 1, Page 101

NAMES: Wife - none named in will and he evidently died sine prolle.
All my debts and funeral charges to be paid by my executor.
No heirs named in will.
Executor: Thomas Pitman
Witnesses: Thomas Beard — /s/ Willm (∅) Moss
John Curry
William Thomson
Will dated 5 March 1753 — Recorded 7 Aug. 1753

Will Book 1, Page 102

Inventory and appraisal of the goods and chattels of the estate of William Moss, deceased, as brought to view, made 27 August 1753 by Willm (W) Verdiman, Joseph Miller and Robert Allen - value 20 pounds 11 shillings 9 pence.

Recorded 4 Sept. 1753

FRANCIS, John — Will Book 1, Page 103

Inventory and appraisal of the estate of John Francis, deceased, made by Owen (O) Sullivant, Thomas Jones and Thos Worthy - value 33 pounds 16 shillings 8 pence.
Recorded 4 Sept. 1753

COCKE, James Will Book 1, Page 104

An inventory of the estate of James Cocke, deceased,
In Lunenburg County - slaves, stock, chattels including furniture.
In Halifax County - slaves and farm tools.
In Amelia County - slaves and farm tools.
In Cumberland County - 13 head of cattle.
Returned 3 Sept. 1753 by John Jas Dupuy, Jonhn Trabue and Barthow Dupuy, executors.

Recorded 4 Sept. 1753

BLANKS, Thomas Will Book 1, Page 107

A true and perfect inventory of the goods and chattels of Mr. Thoms Blanks, deceased, returned 20 August 1753 by Hannah Cargill.

Recorded 4 Sept. 1753

HAYES, Mark Will Book 1, Page 108

Inventory and appraisal of the estate of Mark Hayes, deceased, late of this County, returned 28 August 1753 by John Curry, Thomas Pitman and Joseph Miller - value 29 pounds 16 shillings 6 pence - additional inventory 3 pounds 7 shillings 1 pence.

Recorded 4 Sept. 1753

ROTTINGBURY, Henry (Henry Rottenberry) Will Book 1, Page 109

NAMES: Wife - Margaret Rottingbury
Son - John Rottingbury - 100 acres of land it being part of the tract of land where he now lives and no more of my estate.
Son - Henry Rottingbury - 100 acres where he now lives and no more.
Son - Richard Rottingbury - 100 acres where he now lives, it being part of the same tract and no more.
Daughter - Martha Rottingbury the plantation where I now live, one feather bed, and no more of my estate.
Son-in-law - John Nipper - one shilling to the intent that he may have no more of my estate.
Wife - Margaret Rottingbury all of the rest of my estate.

Executors: Sons John and Henry Rottingbury
Witnesses: Randall Bracey
Mary Bracey

/s/ Henry Rottingbury

Will dated 27 Nov. 1752 Recorded 4 Sept. 1753

NOBLE, Robert — Will Book 1, Page 110

Inventory and appraisal of the estate of Robert Noble, deceased, made by Philemon Russell, Ja[s] McDaniel and William Allen - no total given. Returned to Court by Fra. Wray, administrator.

Recorded 1 Jan. 1754

WAKELY, William (William Weakley ?) — Will Book 1, Page 112

An inventory and appraisement of the estate of William Wakely, deceased, made 18 October 1753 by David Caldwell, John Logan and Christopher (C) Person. Returned by Robert Weakley, administrator.

Recorded 6 Nov. 1753

BROWN, John — Will Book 1, Page 113

NAMES: Wife - Joan Brown
Son - John Brown all that tract of land I hold in Brunswick County lying on Jack's Branch adjoining Col. Harrison .. being by estimation 240 acres.
Son - Richard Brown one shilling and no more beside what he has already received.
Son - Manoah Brown one shilling and no more beside what has already received.
Son - Jesse Brown first living child that my negro woman Ruth shall have and no more except what he has received.
Daughter - Mary Winham one heifer 3 years old and no more except what she has received.
Grandson - John Caulwell Brown, the son of Valentine, all the land that I hold on the north side of Nelson Creek and one negro boy after the decease of my wife Joan Brown.
Son - Valentine Brown all of the land on the south side of Nelsons Creek with the plantation where I am now living and one negro
Wife - Joan Brown to have possession of plantation during her natural life or widowhood. One negro, all stock and chattels for life or widowhood and then to son Valentine.

Executor: Son Valentine Brown
Witnesses: Tyree Glenn
William Willey

/s/ John Brown

Will dated 22 Aug. 1753 — Recorded 5 Feb. 1754

BAKER, Samuel — Will Book 1, Page 115

Account current of the estate of Samuel Baker, deceased, approved by Lyddal Bacon and Geo. Walton, comm. Ordered to be recorded.

Recorded 5 Feb. 1754

BROWN, John — Will Book 1, Page 116

Inventory of the estate of John Brown, deceased, returned to Court by Valentine Brown.

Recorded 5 March 1754

CHRISTOPHER, Nicholas — Will Book 1, Page 117

NAMES; Wife - Ann Christopher
Son - Jacobus Christopher
Son - William Christopher
Daughters - Mary Fennel, Susanna Toon (Tune)
To wife, Ann Christopher, all ready monies, land, chattels, household goods and moveable property as long as she liveth and after her decease to go to my son Jacobus Christopher.
For want of heirs, my will is that the property falleth to my son William Christopher and heirs.
If after my death, my wife should purchase a negro, then after her death the negro to be sold and the money divided between my sons and my daughters Mary Fennell and Susannah Toon.
Memorandum - It is my will that the little boy, Alexander Howard, shall go to his mother after my decease.

Executor: None named in will
Witnesses: William McConnico
Kezia McConnico /s/ Nicholas Christopher
Jared McConnico

Will dated 11 Feb. 1754 — Recorded 5 March 1754

Note: No executor named in will, and Ann Christopher qualified as administratrix with David Christopher and Jacobus Christopher her securities.

SIMKINS, John — Will Book 1, Page 119

NAMES; Wife - Elizabeth Simkins
Daughter - Mary Wheeler one shilling sterling.
Daughter - Rachel Hog one shilling sterling.
Daughter - Elizabeth Pruit one half of may land, being that part whereon she now lives and two negroes.
Daughter - Susanna Lawson two negroes.

To wife, Elizabeth Simkins, during her natural the other half of my land, tow negroes, stock and household goods.

After her death, daughter Susanna Lawson shall have the said lower part of my land.

Daughters - Sarah and Webby Simkins to each a cow to be delivered to them when they marry or come of age.

The two negroes bequeathed to my wife to go after her death to daughters Elizabeth Pruit and Susanna Lawson - one daughter to take the negroes and pay to other one-half of the valuation. All stock and household goods to go to the said two daughters.

If my wife marries, then one-half of said property to go to wife and other half to said two daughters.

Executors: Wife Elizabeth and son-in-law Michael Pruit
Witnesses: Thompson Harris
Elizabeth Hoar /s/ John (O) Simkins
Thomas Watkins

Will dated 22 Jan. 1754 — Recorded 2 April 1754

FIRTH, Daniel — Will Book 1, Page 121

Inventory and appraisal of the estate of Daniel Firth, deceased, made 16 October 1751 by David Gwinn, Jo^s Perrin and Saml Perrin - value 23 pounds 3 shillings 5 pence - returned to Court by Thos Jones, admin.

Recorded 2 April 1754

Will Book 1, Page 123

Account of sales of the estate of Daniel Firth - total 35 pounds 1 shilling 7 pence - returned to Court by Thos Jones, Admin. Ordered recorded.

Recorded 2 April 1754

GWIN, John — Will Book 1, Page 123

Account current of the estate of John Gwin, deceased, approved by Clem^t Read and Thos Nash, ordered recorded.

Recorded 2 April 1754

HALL, William — Will Book 1, Page 125

NAMES: Wife - not named in will.
Son - Thomas Hall personal property and stock.
Granddaughter - Eliball Hall personal property.
Son - Moses Hall one negro and the rest of my worldly estait (sic).

Executor: None named in will.

Witnesses: Richard Womack /s/ William (O) Hall
Ann (A) Womack

Will dated 12 Jan. 1753 Recorded 6 Aug. 1754

Note: No executor named in will, and Moses Hall qualified as administrator with Thomas Bouldin and Thomas Covington his securities.

MILES, John Will Book 1, Page 126

An account current of the estate of John Miles, deceased - mentions expenses for two eldest children and two youngest children - expense of schooling three children - expense of taking children to Pennsylvania.

Account current settled and adjusted by Thomas Bouldin and Abraham Martin, Gents, and ordered to be recorded.

Recorded 7 Aug. 1754

SIMKINS, John Will Book 1, Page 129

Inventory and appraisal of all of the estate goods and chattels of the estate of John Simkins, deceased, made by William Fuqua, John Fuqua and James Hunt, - value 243 pounds 11 shillings 6 pence - returned to Court by Elizabeth Simkins and Mike Pruit, executors.

Recorded 7 May 1754

FIRTH, Daniel Will Book 1, Page 130

Account of sales made for the estate of Daniel Firth, deceased - total 26 pounds 7 shillings 8 pence - returned by Tho[s] Jones, admin.

Recorded 7 May 1754

ROWLETT, Peter Will Book 1, Page 131

NAMES: Wife - mentioned in will but not by name.
Sons - William, Phillip and John Rowlett
All of my lands to be equally divided among my three sons, but in case of death of any of them before age 21, property to be divided equally between the others.
Son - William two negroes on condition my son is to pay to each of my daughters 15 pounds when they come of age or marry.
As to the rest of my estate, my will is that after my wife's third part is deducted, the remainder shall be equally divided amongst my 5 children (two daughters not named).

Executors: McKarness Goode and Phillip Jones
Witnesses: Peter Johnson

Witnesses: John Elam /s/ Peter (X) Rowlett
Wm Baugh

Will dated 11 Jan. 1754 Recorded 7 May 1754

Note: Executors named refused to qualify and Elizabeth Rowlett, relict of said Peter Rowlett, qualified as administrator with will annexed with George Walton her security.

ROWLETT, Peter Will Book 1, Page 132

Inventory and appraisal of the estate of Peter Rowlett, deceased, made 22 June 1754 by William Watkins, Philip Jones and Francis Moor Petty - value 95 pounds 4 shillings 10 pence - returned to Court by Elizabeth Rowlett, administratrix, and ordered recorded.

Recorded 2 July 1754

EDDINS, William Will Book 1, Page 133

NAMES: Wife - Rebecca Eddins
Sons - Jacob, Benjamin and Theophilus Eddins one certain tract of land containing 400 acres, being the dwelling plantation where I now live to be equally divided, except son Theophilus in his part the manor plantation with all improvements thereon.
Son - Isaac Eddins given cows, pigs and feather bed.
Daughter - Mary Eddins one feather bed.
To sons Jacob, Benjamin and Theophilus and daughter Mary all of my estate real and personal.
Son - John Eddins one shilling sterling.
Son - Joseph Eddins one shilling sterling.
Son - Abraham Eddins one shilling sterling.
Son - William Eddins one shilling sterling.
Daughter - Elizabeth Eddins one shilling sterling.
Daughter - Rebecca Eddins one shilling sterling.
Daughter-in-law - Anne Eddins to be enjoyed by her quietly and peacefully during her natural life one certain settlement of land adjoining my manor plantation for her and her children, but if she marries again the legacy to be void.
To wife, Rebecca Eddins, all of the rest of my estate, both real and personal, for her natural life, but if she marries the estate to revert to the use of my children named.

Executors: Wife Rebecca and son Joseph Eddins
Witnesses: John Bailey
William Cross   /s/ William (W) Eddins
Joseph Davey
Will dated 2 Feb. 1754   Recorded 6 Aug. 1754

CURTILLAR, Matthew   Will Book 1, Page 135

NAMES: Wife - Lucy Curtillar
Brother - Abraham Curtillar
Isaac Browne - makes bequest to him.
Mentions unborn child.
If child dies without heirs, land to be divided between John Curtillar and Edward Curtillar. (Connection not stated)(Apparently brothers)
Personal property to be divided between wife Lucy and (unborn) child.
Land left to wife Lucy for life and at her death to child.
Executors: Wife Lucy, father Edward Curtillar and Israel Browne.
Witnesses: John Curtillar   /s/ Matthew (M) Curtillar
Lucy Curtillar
Israel Browne
Will dated 25 March 1754   Recorded 3 Sept. 1754

Note: Edward Curtillar and Israel Browne refused to accept executorship and wife Lucy Curtillar qualified with Edward Curtillar and Israel Browne her securities.

CLISWELL, Uriah   Will Book 1, Page 136

Inventory and appraisal of the estate of Uriah Cliswell deceased, made by James Mackdaniel, John Williams and James Arnoll - value 19 pounds 16 shillings 11 pence - returned to Court.

Recorded 3 Sept. 1754

ROTTENBERRY, Henry   Will Book 1, Page 136

Inventory and appraisal of the estate of Henry Rottenberry, deceased, made 27 Sept. 1754 by John Lankford, Henry Lankford and Tho[s] Wix, returned to Court - value 35 pounds 11 shillings.

Recorded 1 Oct. 1754

EDDINS, William   Will Book 1, Page 137

Inventory and appraisal of the estate of William Eddins deceased, made 3 Jan. 1755 by John Williams, Reps Jones and Robert Leverritt - value 47 pounds 15 shillings 6 pence - returned to Court.

Recorded 11 Jan. 1755

ROYAL, Joseph — Will Book 1, Page 138

Inventory and appraisal of the estate of Joseph Royal, deceased, made by Thos. Moore, John Robertson and Joseph (R) Rud - value 69 pounds 15 shillings 9 pence.
Recorded 7 Jan. 1755

CUTILLO, Matthew (Curtillar) — Will Book 1, Page 139

Inventory and appraisal of the estate of Matthew Curtillar made by John Williams, Phileman Russell and George Green - value 17 pounds 3 shillings 6 pence.
Recorded 7 Jan. 1755

MITCHELL, John — Will Book 1, Page 140

NAMES: Wife - not named in will and evidently deceased.
Son - James Mitchell one pair spoon moulds.
Daughter - Catherine Mitchell, wife of Robert Mitchell, slave and personal property but to go to her son John Mitchell at age 21.
Daughter - Mary Yarbrough a book, wife of William Yarbrough.
Son-in-law - Jacob Mitchell negro and carpenters tools.
Son - Isaac Mitchell shoemakers and cooper's tools.
Housekeeper - Elizabeth Sawyer furniture and stock, other personal property.
Executors: Jacob Mitchell and Isaac Mitchell
Witnesses: Reuben Searcy
Frances (FJ) James /s/ John Mitchell
Ann (∅) James
Will dated 29 Dec. 1753 — Recorded 2 Feb. 1755

YOUNG, Lemuel — Will Book 1, Page 141

Inventory and appraisal of the estate of Lemuel Young, deceased, made 3 Jan. 1755 by Edward Goode, Joseph Greer and Joseph Gill - value 9 pounds 6 shillings 6 pence - returned to Court.
Recorded 4 Feb. 1755

COCKE, James — Will Book 1, Page 142

Inventory of the estate of James Cocke, deceased, in Henrico County - moveable property, slaves, tools and one still - no value given - returned by John James Dupuy, John Trabue and Barth° Bupuy, executors.
Recorded 4 March 1755

COCKE, James Will Book 1, Page 142

Memorandum that Mrs. Cocke has the use of the land and slaves and all things mentioned in this inventory as long as she lives.

Additional inventory of the estate of James Cocke, deceased:
To cash received from Thomas Anderseon, Lunenburg Co. 19 pounds 6 shillings.
To cash received from Robert Williams, Lunenburg Co. for hire (slaves) 2 pounds 18 shillings.
To cash received from John Pleasant at Baley's Run, Henrico County 4 pounds 14 shillings 8 pence.
Balance due from Elexander Mackie for tobacco sold him by James Cocke 282 pounds 9 shillings 10 pence.
Crop of tobacco made in year 1753 in Lunenburg, Halifax and Amelia Counties - 27592 pounds.
97 Brl corn in Lunenburg County for use of negroes in Halifax County.
113 Brl corn for use of negroes in Amelia County.
178 Brl corn and 78 bu 3 pecks wheat.
Returned by John James Dupuy, John Trabue and Bartho Dupuy, executors.

Recorded 4 March 1755

MITCHELL, John Will Book 1, Page 144

Appraisal of the estate of John Mitchell, deceased, ordered at Feb. Court 1755, Lunenburg County, made by Pinkth Hawkins, Thos Eastland and Jas Coleman - moveable property valued at 69 pounds 8 shillings 11½ pence.

Recorded 1 April 1755

CHRISTOPHER, Nicholas Will Book 1, Page 145

A true and perfect inventory of the estate of Nichs Christopher, deceased - value 76 pounds 6 shillings 1 pence - returned to Court by Anna Christopher, adminx.

Recorded 1 April 1755

OSBORNE, Thomas Will Book 1, Page 146

A true inventory of the estate of Thos Osborn, deceased made by Wm Goode, William Harris and Macarness Goode - Piece of Gold 2 pounds 11 shillings 10½ pence - other property 11 pounds 6 shillings 5½ pence - returned by Robt Wooding, administrator.

Recorded 1 April 1755

SULLIVANT, John — Will Book 1, Page 147

Account current of the estate of John Sullivant, deceased, returned by Charles Sullivant - approved and settled by Clem Read and Tho Nash.

Recorded 1 April 1755

A true inventory of part of the estate of John Sullivant, deceased, taken by Wilson Mattox and Henry Isbell - value 6 pounds o shillings 0 pence, - returned by Charles Sullivant.

Recorded 1 April 1755

HUDSON, John — Will Book 1, Page 148

Appraisal of the estate of John Hudson, deceased, made by Robert Coleman, Nicholas Major and Anthony Hughes, - value 7 pounds 2 shillings 9 pence - ordered recorded.

Recorded 3 June 1755

TWITTY, John — Will Book 1, Page 149

Inventory and appraisal of the estate of John Twitty, lately deceased, made by Christopher Hudson, Joseph Ragsdale and John Hyde - value 21 pounds 15 shillings 6 pence.

Recorded 5 July 1755

Account of sales of the estate of John Twitty, deceased made 5 July 1755 - 21 pounds 6 shillings 4 pence.

Recorded 5 Aug. 1755

BERRY, John (John Barry ?) — Will Book 1, Page 150

The remainess (sic) part of the estate of John Berry, deceased, valued by us Rich[d] Seat and Reps Jones - two mares 3 pounds 15 shillings - an old broad Ax 2 shillings 6 pence.

Recorded 5 Aug. 1755

WRIGHT, John — Will Book 1, Page 150

An inventory of the estate of Jno Wright, deceased, made by George Baskervill, Hutchens Burton and Dennis Larke - value 78 pounds 9 shillings 6 pence
Additional inventory of the estate of Jno Wright, dec. - value 193 pounds 1 shilling 9 pence - returned to Court by John Speed, administrator.

Recorded 3 Sept. 1755

WILLIAMS, John — Will Book 1, Page 152

Inventory and appraisal of the estate of John Williams deceased, made 6 Sept. 1755 by Rich[d] Leak, Robert

Moore, Senr., and Robert Moore, Junr. - no value given. And

an account of sales of the estate of John Williams, deceased, made 27 Sept. 1755 - no total given - returned to Court by Mary Williams and James Moore - ordered recorded.

Recorded 4 Nov. 1755

WILLIAMSON, Thomas — Will Book 1, Page 154

NAMES: Wife - Martha Jones Williamson
Children - mentioned but not by name.
Bequest - To wife Martha Jones Williamson all personal estate for life.
Lend to wife a negro, plantation and adjoining land.
I desire all my lands to be divided among my children - Executors to divide land as children come to the age of maturity.

Executors: Cap[n] Thomas Bouldin, James Hunt, Joseph Williams and Memucan Hunt

Witnesses: Richard Ward
Peter Hudson
Henrietta Williams
Jos. Williams

/s/ Tho[s] Williamson

Will dated 25 June 1755 — Recorded 7 Oct. 1755

Note: Joseph Williams, Gent., qualified as executor with Thomas Nash, William Jones, John Cox and William Petty Pool his securities.

EVANS, Morris — Will Book 1, Page 155

Inventory and appraisal of the estate of Morris Evans, deceased, made by Samuel Holmes, Samuel Manning and Ephraim Mabry - value 5 pounds 9 shillings 11 pence - returned to Court by Wm Poole.

Recorded 2 June 1756

FREEMAN, Arthur — Will Book 1, Page 156

Inventory and appraisal of the estate of Arthur Freeman deceased, made 3 Oct. 1753 by David Garland, Phill[m] Russell and Henry Gill - value 175 pounds 5 shillings 1 pence.

Additional inventory and appraisal made 7 Dec. 1753 by John Wilburn, Henry Freeman, W[m] Richardson and Daniel Knight - value 54 pounds 10 shillings 3 pence.

Recorded 1 June 1756

CHILES, Henry — Will Book 1, Page 158

NAMES: Wife - mentioned in will but not by name

Daughter - Elizabeth Chiles
Mentions unborn child
Mother - mentioned in will but not by name.
Father - mentioned in will but not by name.
Grandmother - Mary Howl
Mentions land left to him by the will of his father after the death of his mother (living).
Refers to property coming to him after the death of his grandmother.

Executors: Wife (not named), Philleman Russell and David Garland

Witnesses: James Stewart /s/ Henry Chiles
William Mills

Will dated 6 March 1756 Recorded 6 July 1756

RODGERS, Andrew Will Book 1, Page 160

Names: Wife - Janet Rodgers
Sons - Andrew and John Rodgers
Bequest - To sons Andrew and John Rodgers tract of land where I now live to be divided between them - containg 373 acres.
Son - Thomas Patrick Rodgers one shilling.
Daughter - Rebecah Rodgers one shilling.
Daughter - Margret Anderson one shilling.
Daughter - Elizabeth Culbertson one shilling.
Daughter - Martha Burnside one shilling.
Mentions orphan child, Rachel Muntlin - living with him.
Wife Janet to have property for life or widowhood.

Executors: Wife Janet Rodgers and son-in-law James Burnside

Witnesses: David Caldwell /s/ Andrew (AR) Rodgers
William Cunningham
Wm Caldwell

Will dated 18 Dec. 1755 Recorded 6 July 1756

RODGERS, Andrew Will Book 1, Page 162

Inventory of the estate of Andrew Rodgers, deceased, made by Robert Andrews, Jacob Robison and John East - no totals given.

Recorded 4 Nov. 1756

WEATHERFORD, Richard Will Book 1, Page 163

NAMES: Wife - none named in will and evidently deceased
Son - John Weatherford plantation by estimation 800 acres and all other goods and chattels

Executor: None named in will

Witnesses: James Mackdaniel
John Tomson /s/ Richard (R) Weatherford
Charles (C) Weatherford

Will dated 12 Nov. 1755 | Recorded 6 July 1756

JUSTICE, Justinia | Will Book 1, Page 163

Names: Wife - Mary Justice
Bequest - To wife Mary one-third of estate.
Daughters - Elizabeth Justice, Sarah Justice, Mary Justice
Bequest - Remaining two-thirds of estate.
Executors to make a lawful deed for 100 acres of land to William Justice, Junr., in the County of Charles City.
Executors: Wife Mary Justice and Isaac Johnston
Witnesses: Wm Scott
Samuel Davies
William Johnston
/s/ Justinia (J) Justice

Will dated 1 Oct. 1755 | Recorded 3 Aug. 1756

ALLEN, Joel | Will Book 1, Page 165

NAMES: Wife - Mary Allen
Daughter - Susanna Allen
Bequest - To daughter Susanna 30 pounds when she becomes age 18 or marries.
To wife Mary all remainder of estate after payment of debts.
Executors: Wife Mary Allen and Richard Scruggs
Witnesses: William Roberts
William Matthews
/s/ Joel Allen

Will dated 29 July 1756 | Recorded 7 Dec. 1756

COCKE, James | Will Book 1, Page 166

Account current of the estate of Mr. James Cocke, deceased, (account six pages - mentions that "carried corps of James Cocke from Lunenburg to Malvern Hill in Henrico County") - account returned by John James Dupuy, John Trabue and Barth^o Dupuy.

Account settled and adjusted by Clem^t Read, Jas. Taylor and Thos Nash.

Recorded 2 Sept. 1755

DABBS, Joseph | Will Book 1, Page 172

Account current of the estate of Joseph Dabbs, deceased adjusted 5 Aug. 1754 by Thomas Bouldin and Thos Nash, examiners. Executors had to put money to balance the account.

Recorded 1 Oct. 1754

SAWYERS, Elizabeth | Will Book 1, Page 176

Appraisal of the estate of Elizabeth Sawers, deceased,

made by Jacob Mitchell, George Farrar and Isaac Mitchell - value 12 pounds 16 shillings 11 ½ pence - returned to Court by Thos. Stevens.

Recorded 1 March 1757

BROOKS, Richard   Will Book 1, Page 177

Repps Jones, Drury Moor and Hugh Wyley were sworn before Capn Jinings, one of His Majestys Justices to appraise and value in current money the estate of Richard Brooks, deceased. - value 27 pounds 5 shillings 3 pence.

Recorded 1 March 1757

ELLIS, Jeremiah   Will Book 1, Page 178

NAMES: Wife - Priscilla Ellis
Daughter - Priscilla Nipper two cows, pewter basin
Daughter - Lydia Nipper two cows, pewter basin
Daughter - Ann Mulkey 2 cows
Daughter - Joanna Ellis two cows and pewter
Daughter - Mary Murfey pewter
Son - Abraham Ellis tract of land in my lower survey.
Son - Nathan Ellis land adjoining Abraham Ellis
Son - James Ellis land adjoining Nathan Ellis and adjoining plantation where I now live.
Youngest son - Daniel Ellis all rest of my land with the plantation.
All of the rest of my personal estate to wife Priscilla and at her death to be divided among my five daughters, Mary, Priscilla, Lydia, Ann and Joanna.

Executor: Wife Priscilla Ellis

Witnesses: Jno Esel (Ezell), Junr.
Benja Harrison
Wm Douglas   /s/ Jeremiah (ɪ) Ellis
Will   Julius Nichols

Will dated 13 Nov. 1756   Recorded 3 May 1757

DRUMRIGHT, James   Will Book 1, Page 181

Inventory and appraisal of the estate of James Drumright, deceased, made 18 Jan. 1757 by Nath Garland, John Williams and John Bacon - value 12 pounds 8 shillings 6 3/4 pence.

Recorded 3 May 1757

COCKERHAM, Henry   Will Book 1, Page 182

NAMES: Wife - mentioned in will but not by name.
Son - Henry Cockerham land lying in the fork of Blackstone Creek.
Son - William Cockerham my dwelling house and the

lands belonging thereto.
Daughter - Frances Cockerham personal property.
Daughter - Susannah Cockerham personal property.
Rest of my goods and chattels to my wife for widowhood or life, but if she marries again to be divided among my children.

Executors: Wife (not named) and John Hix
Witnesses: John Hix
John Smith /s/ Henry Cockerham
Moses Cockerham

Will dated 19 Sept. 1754 Recorded 3 May 1757

COCKERHAM, Henry Will Book 1, Page 183

Inventory and appraisal of the estate of Henry Cockerham ordered 3 May 1757, made 3 June 1757 by Tyree Glenn, Robert Brooks and John Scott - value 136 pounds 17 shillings 5 pence.

Recorded 7 June 1957

DAVIS, John Will Book 1, Page 185

Order of March Court 1757 to appraise the estate of Mr. John Davis - made by Richard Fox, Thomas Stevens and John Blanton - value 1370 pounds 0 shillings 2 pence.

Recorded 7 June 1757

WILLIAMSON, Thomas Will Book 1, Page 189

Appraisal of the estate of John Williamson, deceased, made by Stephen Wood, Isaac Johnson and Joseph Johnson, Senr. - value 82 pounds 1 shilling 4 pence.

Recorded 7 June 1757

ELLIS, Jeremiah Will Book 1, Page 191

A true inventory of the goods and chattels of the estate of Jeremiah Ellis, deceased, made by Gabriel Harden W Douglas and Stephen Jones - value 64 pounds 10 shillings 10 pence - returned to Court by Priscilla Ellis, executrix.

Recorded 2 Aug. 1757

FARMER, Benjamin Will Book 1, Page 193

NAMES: Wife - Sarah Farmer
Bequest - To wife Sarah plantation, stock and all of my estate for life or widowhood
Son - Benjamin Farmer 200 acres at the upper part of my land.
Son - John Farmer plantation and 200 acres of land (for which) he is to maintain his mother as long as she lives.

Son - Isom (Isham) Farmer 280 acres of land on Staunton River.
Daughter - Sarah Farmer side saddle after her mother's decease, (then) all household goods and stock to be divided among all of my children.
If either of my sons die before they come of age, their lot is to be divided among all.
Executors: Thomas Bouldin, John Farmer, Thomas Bedford and Mark Farmer
Witnesses: Henry Childers
John Childers /s/ Benjamin Farmer
James Foord
Will dated 2 June 1757 Recorded 2 Aug. 1757

JONES, David Will Book 1, Page 195

Inventory and appraisal of the estate of David Jones, deceased, made 28 July 1757 by Thomas Bouldin and George Foster - value 14 pounds 14 shillings 9 pence.
Recorded 2 Aug. 1757

AVRETH, Thomas (Thomas Averett) Will Book 1, Page 196

NAMES: Wife - mentioned in will but not by name, wife Sarah named as an executrix.
Son - Thomas Avreth land whereon I now live
Sons - Henry, William, Matthew and Isham Avreth My survey of 380 acres of land to be divided between them.
Son - James Avreth one heifer
Son - John Avreth one heifer
Son - Thomas Avreth one heifer
Grandson - James Wilkins son of my daughter Sarah Wilkins one cow.
Grandson - Bucknah Smith son of my daughter Elizabeth Smith one heifer.
The rest of my estate to my wife during her life or widowhood and then to be divided equally between all of my children.
Executors: Wife Sarah and son Thomas Avreth
Witnesses: Gideon Crenshaw and Matthew Tanner
/s/ Thomas (T) Avreth
Will dated 20 Jan. 1751 Recorded 6 Sept. 1757

Note: Thomas Avreth qualified as executor with Thomas Hawkins and Thomas Moore his securities.

COCKE, James Will Book 1, Page 199

Current account of the estate of James Cocke, deceased, returned to Court by John James Dupuy, John Trabue and Bartho Dupuy, executors. Account examined and approved by Clem Read, Jas. Taylor and Thomas Bouldin 5 Sept.

1757 and ordered to be recorded (consists of 10 pages)
Recorded 6 Sept. 1757

DAVIS, John — Will Book 1, Page 209

An inventory of part of the estate of Mr. Jno. Davis made by Rich[d] Fox, Thomas Stevens and Jn[o] Blanton, returned to Court by W[m] Davis, administrator.
No total given. Recorded Oct. Court 1757

POOL, Thomas — Will Book 1, Page 209

An inventory of the estate of Thomas Pool, deceased, made 28 March 1757 by Thomas Eastland, Matthew Tanner and John Glass - value 29 pounds 17 shillings 11½ pence - returned to Court by Thos. Anderson, admin.
Recorded 1 Nov. 1757

AVORY, Thomas — Will Book 1, Page 210

Apraisal of the estate of Thomas Avory, deceased, made by John Roberson, Joseph Rud and Matthew Tanner - no value given - returned to Court by Thomas Avory, admin.
Recorded 1 Nov. 1757

CALDWELL, James — Will Book 1, Page 211

NAMES: Wife - Elizabeth Caldwell
Bequest - To wife Elizabeth all my personal estate except what I shall further bequeath.
Son - George Caldwell my plantation including 155 acres of land when he is of age except that the land shall continue in my wife's possession during (her) life.
Son - James Caldwell 155 acres of land being part of ye tract I now live on including his house and improvements.
Son - John Caldwell 155 acres on the side of the tract I now live on and on both sides of the new road.
Son-in-law - George Scot part of tract of land he now lives on and my executor to give him a deed.
To Samuel Daves the lower part of the tract of land George Scot lives on.
To James Perton one English shilling.
To Joseph Ironmonger one English shilling.
To Thomas Vernon one English shilling.
To William Scot one English shilling.
To Nehemiah and Joseph Vernon, sons of Isaack Vernon one pound each.
I leave to my wife during her life Henry Cald-

well, an orphan child, and then to my son James for the remainder of this servitude.

Executors: Wife Elizabeth and son James Caldwell
Witnesses: John Pamplin
Samuel Davies /s/ James Caldwell
Robert Woods

Will dated 10 Aug. 1757 Recorded 6 Dec. 1757

STEPHENS, Thomas (Thomas Stevens) Will Book 1. Page 215

A just and true inventory of the estate of Tho Stephens, deceased, taken by George Farrar, Edm Bugg and James Cocke - value 32 pounds 5 shillings 9 pence - returned to Court by Mary Stephens, adminx.

Recorded 5 June 1758

HOBSON, Nicholas Will Book 1, Page 216

NAMES: Wife - Agnes Hobson
Son - John Hobson 400 acres of land in Lunenburg County on branches of the Meherrin River to include the houses where John Baker now lives.
Son - Matthew Hobson 290 acres on the Roanoke River adjoining the line of Tandy Walker, deceased, and 400 acres on Meherrin River adjoining Hawkins, negro and personal property.
Son - Nicholas Hobson one-half of the 880 acres where on my dwelling house is and 400 acres at the lower plantation and personal property.
Son - William Hobson one-half of the aforesaid land where my dwelling house is ... to be divided by my executors and William to have the upper part where my dwelling is and Nicholas the lower part.
Daughter - Obedience Bacon 400 acres of land adjoining John Hobson.
Daughter - Agnes Bacon 490 acres of land lying on the branches of Laton's Creek adjoining James Bilbo.
Daughter - Sarah Hobson 600 acres of land lying on the branches of the Meherrin River
Daughter - Margrata Hobson 250 acres of land adjoining Obedience and Sarah, and personal property.
Grandson - Nicholas Bilbo 250 acres of land adjoining Margrata and Sarah Hobson.
Wife - Agnes Hobson the plantation I live on as long as she lives a widow and negroes, and at her death to be sold and divided among my five youngest children.

Daughter - Elizabeth Bugg one cow and calf.
Rest of my property, both real and personal, to my wife.

Executors: Son John Hobsom, wife Agnes Hobson and Edward Goode

Witnesses: Wm Stone /s/ Nicholas (X) Hobson
Jeremiah Hatcher
William McDow

Will dated 25 May 1758 Recorded 5 Dec. 1758

EVANS, Morris Will Book 1, Page 219

An account of the estate of Morris Evans, deceased, sold by William Poole - no total given - examined and approved by John Speed and Henry Delony 20 July 1758.
Recorded 1 Aug. 1758

WEATHERFORD, Susanna Will Book 1, Page 220

(Susanna Weatherford otherwise Waller of Lunenburg County)

NAMES: Daughter - Lucy Parsons - Clothes, furniture and what is due of a hogshead of tobacco allowed to me by the Vestry of Hanover Parish.

Executor: Christopher Parsons

Witnesses: James Rutherford /s/ Susanna (X) Weatherford
Rose Rutherford

Will dated 18 Dec. 1756 Recorded 4 July 1758

WILBURN, John Will Book 1, Page 222

NAMES: Wife - mentioned in will but not by name.
Children - mentioned in will but not by name.
I leave all my lands and personal estate to be sold to pay my just debts.
If there is personal estate enough, my land not to be sold.
To my wife all remainder of my estate, after payment of debts, to bring up my children

Executors: Friends John Camp and William Harris

Witnesses: William Harris
Richard (I) Hudson /s/ John (J) Wilburn
Hugh (EM) Mackvay

Will dated 18 Aug. 1757 Recorded 7 March 1758

PINSON, Aaron, Senr. Will Book 1, Page 223

NAMES: Wife - none named in will and evidently deceased
Son - Aaron Pinson 100 acres of land (part of) my land whereon I now live.
Son - Thomas Pinson 150 acres being part of the

land where I now live.
Son - John Pinson 150 acres of land adjoining land where I now live.
Son Thomas Pinson horses and cattle - the mare the gift of his Godfather Christopher Ranbury.
Daughter - Elinor Pinson horses and cattle they being the gift of her Godfather Christopher Ranbury.
Grandson - Moses Grigg a cow and calf when he comes of age.
Anything left, after worldly contracts are discharged, to be divided among all of my children.

Executors: Sons Aaron and Thomas Pinson
Witnesses: Henry Philip Hart
William Royster
Stephen Wiles

/s/ Aaron (A) Pinson

Will dated 26 Dec. 1757 — Recorded 7 March 1758

PINSON, Aaron — Will Book 1, Page 225

Inventory of the estate of Aaron Pinson, deceased, made 28 March 1758 by John Jones, Owen (O) Franklin and William (X) Colbreath - value not stated.

Recorded 4 April 1758

WILBURN, John — Will Book 1, Page 227

Appraisement of the estate of John Wilburn, deceased, taken 17 March 1758 by Jn° Camp, John Jeffries and Richd Swepson - no total given.

Recorded 4 April 1758

CRENSHAW, Joseph — Will Book 1, Page 228

NAMES: Wife - not named in will and deceased. No
Eldest son - William Crenshaw 5 pounds sterling
Son - Gideon Crenshaw 5 pounds current money
Son - Joseph Crenshaw 30 shillings current money
Daughter - Priscilla Duke feather bed and furniture.
Daughter - Hannah Barkman feather bed and cover, horse and other personal property.
"If Hannah's husband comes to entice away what I have given her, I give it to my daughter Mary Cook."
Youngest son - Micajah Crenshaw land where I now live, horse, saddle and personal property.
I desire that son Micajah shall be under the care of his brother Thomas.
To my wife the liberty of the plantation during the time of her widowhood.
The rest of my estate to be equally divided be-

tween all of my children except my son William who has his share.

I desire that my estate be not appraised.

Executors: Sons Thomas and Gideon Crenshaw

Witnesses: Gideon Crenshaw
William (W) Wilkins /s/ Jos Crenshaw
Ann (X) Wilson

Will dated 1757 Recorded 14 Oct. 1758

CARGILL, Hannah Will Book 1, Page 230

NAMES: Husband - Cornelius Cargill
Bequest: Cattle and sheep
God-daughter - Elizabeth Drew - given two sheep.
Son - William Blanks - bequest of all furniture that belongs to me and personal property.
Grandson - Thomas Blanks, son of William Blanks by his present wife Judith - given cow and calf.
Son - Richard Blanks - personal property.

Executors: Sons William and Richard Blanks

Witnesses: Wm Roberts
John Cargill /s/ Hannah (S) Cargill
Thomas Dendy

Will dated 7 Nov. 1757 Recorded 4 April 1758

Richard Blanks qualified as executor with James Burton and James Hudson his securities.

FARMER, Benjamin Will Book 1, Page 232

An account of the sales of the estate of Benjamin Farmer, deceased - total 88 pounds 10 shillings 11 pence - returned to Court by Sarah S. Farmer, adminx.

Recorded 6 June 1758

FARMER, Benjamin Will Book 1, Page 234

Inventory and appraisal of the estate of Benjamin Farmer, deceased, made by John Townes, Thomas Ligon and Stephen Bedford - value 92 pounds 17 shillings 10 pence - returned to Court by Sarah S. Farmer, adminx.

Recorded 6 June 1758

HILL, Richard Will Book 1, Page 236

An account of the sales of the estate of Richard Hill, deceased - no total given.

Recorded 6 June 1758

CALDWELL, James — Will Book 1, Page 237

Inventory and appraisal of the estate of James Caldwell, deceased, made by Thomas Vernon, John Logan, James Barton and James Murphey - value 46 pounds 19 shillings 9 pence.
Test: William Caldwell — Recorded 6 June 1758

HILL, Richard — Will Book 1, Page 239

Pursuant to an order of Court, we have appraised the estate of Richard Hill, deceased - value 14 pounds 17 shillings 3 pence - /s/ W[m] Watkins, Francis More Petty, Thomas M. Mitchell, Michael M. Gill.
Recorded 6 June 1758

YOUNG, John — Will Book 1, Page 241

Inventory and appraisal of the estate of John Young, deceased, made 30 June 1748 by Thomas Jones, Abra: Martin, David Givin, Thomas Bouldin - value 13 pounds 19 shillings 9 pence.
Returned to Court by Elizabeth O. Young
Recorded 4 July 1758

McCONNICO, William — Will Book 1, Page 240

An inventory and appraisal of the estate of William McConnico, deceased - value 220 pounds 7 shillings 7 pence.
Recorded 1 Aug. 1758

DAVID, Adlar — Will Book 1, Page 242

An inventory and appraisal of the estate of Adlar David made pursuant to order of Court July ye 5th 1749 by Luke Smith, Senr., Peter Hutson and Edward Parke - value 233 pounds 8 shillings - returned to Court by Sam[l] Harris, Executor, 7 Aug. 1749.
Recorded 5 Oct. 1749

MOREFIELD, John — Will Book 1, Page 244

NAMES: Wife - not named and deceased
Daughter - Jane Morefield
Grandson - John Morefield
Leaves to daughter and grandson "the land I now live on".
Daughter - Elizabeth Morefield
Leaves to daughters Jane and Elizabeth Morefield "all of my livestock and furniture".
Executors: Daughters Jane and Elizabeth Morefield

Witnesses:
Thomas Blanks /s/ John (I) Morefield
Elleckzander Straingе
Will dated 13 May 1751 Recorded 3 Oct. 1751

Executors named qualified with John Ashworth and Thomas Blanks their securities.

HARWOOD, George Will Book 1, Page 245

NAMES: Wife - mentioned in will but not by name
Son - Francis Harwood - eldest son
Bequest - Plantation "where I now live" containing 274 acres to "my oldest son Francis Harwood"
"But I order that my wife have full possession of the same during her widowhood, and if she marry after my son arrives at the age 18 then I order that she have the third of the said plantation during her lifetime for the support of my other children" (not named).
Bequest: To son Francis - a young mare.
Plantation on Ward's Fork to be sold and titled by my executors.
After payment of debts, my wife to have all personal property for support of my <u>four</u> children.
At the death of my wife, property to be divided at the discretion of my executors.

Executors: David Caldwell and John Logan
Witnesses:
David Logan /s/ George (H) Harwood
Ashworth Middleton
Will dated 13 Jan. 1750/1 Recorded 3 April 1751

DAY, Thomas Will Book 1, Page 247

An account current of the estate of Thomas Day, deceased, returned by Nicholas Hayle, administrator.
Recorded 3 Oct. 1750

ALLEN, Charles, Senr. Will Book 1, Page 247

NAMES: Wife - not named in will
Daughter - Sarah Stokes - 5 shillings
Daughter - Mary Allem - 50 pounds and a bed to be paid her if she lives to be of age
Granddaughter - Susannah Allen - 20 pounds to be paid her if she lives to be of age.
Son - Charles Allen - All lands and personal property.

Executor: Son Charles Allen, Junr.

Witnesses:
Robert Mann
Richard Blanks
William Green

/s/ Char[les] Allen

Will dated 8 April 1758 — Recorded 3 April 1759

Charles Allen, Junr., qualified as executor with Pinkethman Hawkins his security.

WILLIS, John — Will Book 1, Page 248

Inventory and appraisal of the estate of John Willis, deceased, made 2nd day of December 1758 by John Ballard Howell Collier and David Dortch, returned to Court by William Lucas, administrator.

Recorded 2 May 1759

BUGG, Samuel, Senr. — Will Book 1, Page 249

NAMES: Wife - Sarah Bugg
Son - Jacob Bugg - negro
Daughter - Sarah Towler - negro and after her death to her children
Daughter - Agnes Lee - negro
Daughter - Ruth Bugg - negro and furniture
Son - Sherwood Bugg - 10 pounds money
Grandsons - John, Benjamin, Jesse and Sherwood Bugg - 10 pounds money each
Son - Edmund Bugg - livestock
Son - Samuel Bugg - 20 shillings Sterling
Son - Anselm Bugg - all of my land and all of the remainder of my estate both real and personal
Lend all of my estate to my wife Sarah during her natural life, and at her decease to be divided as stated.

Executor: Son Anselm Bugg
Witnesses:
Amos Hix
George Freeman
William Cox

/s/ Samuel (ß) Bugg

Will dated 13 Dec. 1756 — Recorded 1 May 1759

Anselm Bugg qualified as executor with Samuel Young and Sherwood Bugg his securities.

HAWKINS, Thomas — Will Book 1, Page 250

NAMES: Wife - Mary Hawkins
Son - Matthew Hawkins
Son - John Hawkins
Daughter - Sarah Hawkins

Bequest - To wife Mary six negroes for life and then to son Matthew Hawkins

To son Matthew the plantation where I now live containing all the lands I bought of William Thomason, James Parrish and John Clarke, except I leave to my wife her third of same during her life.

Bequest - To son John a plantation in North Carolina on Island Creek.

Bequest - Slaves to sons Matthew and John Hawkins

Bequest - Slaves to daughter Sarah Hawkins

Bequest - To unborn child - slaves

To John Clarke 200 acres of land on Sandy Creek provided that he makes my heir a right to the land I bought of him on the north side of Butchers Creek.

Bequest: - If unborn child is a boy, he shall have the lands in dispute between Stephens Collins and I if recovered. If not, I leave him 600 acres on Grassy Creek in North Carolina.

All of the rest of my lands to be sold.

Executors: My brother Pink(ethman) Hawkins and my wife Mary Hawkins

Leave to John Potter 30 pounds to collect in my Sheriff's arears.

Witnesses:

Joseph Dobson Joseph Rudd
Matthew Turner
Martha Jarrot
Jacob (I) Coleson

/s/ Thomas Hawkins

Will dated 14 Nov. 1758 — Recorded 1 May 1759

Executors named qualified with Joseph Williams, Joseph Truman, William Caldwell, Samuel Young and James Easter their securities.

FLINN, Loflin — Will Book 1, Page 252

NAMES: Wife - mentioned in will but not by name
Son - James Flinn
Son - George Flinn
Son - John Flinn
Son - Thomas Flinn

Bequest - To sons James and George Flinn my land I now live on to be equally divided between them

After my wife's death, I give to my sons James and George as much of my personal estate as will make them equal with my sons John and Thomas Flinn. All of the rest of my estate to be divided equally among all of my children.

Son Thomas to pay to my estate the account I have against him for 5 pounds 12 shillings 9 pence.

Son George to pay to my estate the account that I have against him for 7 pounds.

The sum of these accounts to be divided equally between all of my children.

God-son - Lawflin - bequest (Lawflin Flinn)

Personal estate to sons John and Thomas, and they are to sell same and divide the proceeds among all of my children.

Executors: Sons John and Thomas Flinn

Witnesses:

Benjamin Ragsdale — /s/ Lawflin (X) Flin

John (X) Tomson

Augustine Rowland

Will dated 24 Sept. 1758 — Recorded 1 May 1759

John Flinn qualified as executor with Thomas Flinn and John Cox his securities.

JONES, Thomas — Will Book 1, Page 254

NAMES: Wife - Amey Jones

Daughter - Elizabeth Jones and her husband Richard Jones

Son - Godfrey Jones

It is my desire that my daughter Elizabeth Jones and her husband Richard Jones, and my son Godfrey Jones keep for themselves all of the estate they are now possessed with as their part of my estate.

Son - David Jones

Son - Thomas Jones

Gives to sons David and Thomas Jones all of the lands I am now possessed with to be divided between them. Gives to son David Jones slaves.

I desire that my son Thomas be bound out to a carpenter's trade.

I desire that my executors give a deed of conveyance in fee simple to James Easter for 200 acres of land where he now lives when the said Easter shall make a deed of conveyance for a certain tract of land containing 300 acres adjoining the land I now live on.

After payment of debts, I desire that the rest of my estate be equally divided between my wife and children, namely, David Jones, Rachel Jones, Thomas Jones, Dorothy Jones, Martha Jones and Mary Jones.

Executors: Wife Amey and sons Godfrey and David Jones

Witnesses: M. Stanfield

Matthew Talbot — /s/ Thos Jones

John Brunskill

Will dated 5 Nov. 1748 — Recorded 6 March 1748/49

LYDDERDALE, William Will Book 1, Page 256

NAMES: Wife - Sarah Lydderdale

Bequest to wife 370 acres of land on the middle fork of Bluestone Creek during her natural life. To my wife the two mares her father gave William (not stated but presumedly a deceased son).

Personal property to be sold together with 50 acres of land adjoining Mr. Thomas Satterwhite to pay my just debts.

After payment of debts, I desire that my estate be equally divided between my two daughters.

Daughter - Wilmouth Lydderdale

Daughter - Sarah Lydderdale

I desire that my daughters be schooled out of my estate.

Executors: My friends Thomas Anderson and David Haliburton

Witnesses:

John S. Lyon /s/ William (W) Lydderdale

Charles S. Lyon

Will dated 11 Jan. 1759 Recorded 5 June 1759

David Haliburton qualified as executor.

Sarah, the widow and relict of the deceased, came into Court and expressed her disapprobation to the said will and renounced all claim by virtue of any bequest in the said will. Certified by Clerk of the Court.

TURNER, Robert Will Book 1, Page 257

Inventory and appraisal of the estate of Robert Turner, deceased, made 10 June 1758 by James Arnold, William Allen and Ruben Vaughan - value 5 pounds 19 shillings 9½ pence.

Recorded 5 June 1759

BACON, John Planter Will Book 1, Page 258

NAMES: Wife - Frances Bacon

Son - John Bacon

Bequest to son John Bacon after death or marriage of my wife, one slave, upon consideration of his paying 30 pounds in two bonds for which I am bound as his security.

Bequest to wife Frances - to have use and occupation of all personal estate not already given for life or widowhood.

Son - Nathaniel Bacon

Son-in-law - Benjamin Estes

My estate, after the decease of my wife, to be divided amongst my children William Bacon, Edmond Bacon, Nathaniel Bacon, Francis Bacon, Elizabeth Bacon, Sarah Bacon, Susannah Bacon and Mary Bacon.

My son Nathaniel shall not receive any part of my estate until he pays 25 pounds he is in debt to me for which I gave him cash.

If ever Benjamin Estes, who married my daughter Frances, is known to play at game or games that whatsoever I have bequeathed to her shall be equally divided among my other children.

My daughter Mary is to have first choice in a division of my estate.

Executors: Wife Frances, son William Bacon and brother Lyddal Bacon

Witnesses:
C. Courtney
Grissell Bacon

/s/ John Bacon

Will dated 20 Oct. 1758 — Recorded 3 July 1759

Frances Bacon qualified as executrix with George Elliott, Lyddal Bacon and John Ragsdale her securities.

RUSSELL, John — Will Book 1, Page 260

Inventory and appraisal of the estate of John Russell, deceased, made 19 June 1759 by Josias Randle, Thomas Taylor and Godfrey Jones, value 7 pounds 6 pence.

Recorded 3 July 1759

COLBREATH, John — Will Book 1, Page 261

NAMES: Wife - Mary Colbreath

Bequest: Wife Mary to peaceably and quietly possess 100 acres together with plantation where I now live for her natural life.

After her decease, land and plantation to go to son John Colbreath.

Son - Daniel Colbreath - 100 acres of wood land on lower side of Grassy Creek.

I desire that my young 3 year old horse to be sold by my executors and money to be laid out in land for my son Joseph Colbreath, but if he dies before age 21 money or land to be equally divided among my living children.

I desire that certain cattle (designated) be sold by my executors and money divided between my daughters Caty and Peggy Colbreath.

All residue of my estate to go to my wife Mary.

Executors: Daniel McNeal and Edward Colbreath

Witnesses:
Richard Yancey — /s/ John (Θ) Colbreath
W^m (X) Colbreath
Wilson Colbreath

Will dated 1 May 1759 — Recorded 7 Aug. 1759

Daniel McNeal qualified as executor with Edward Colbreath his security.

HOLLOWAY, George — Will Book 1, Page 264

NAMES: Wife - not named in will and evidently deceased
Son - William Holloway
Son Bennett Holloway
Son - John Holloway
Son - James Holloway
Son George Holloway
Son Thomas Holloway
Daughter - Dianah Holloway
Daughter - Ann Holloway

Makes specific bequests to each child.

Gives each son 177 acres of land

John Speed, John Ballard, George Farrar and Henry Delony, or any two of them, to divide land given to sons.

Executors: Son Bennett Holloway and Henry Delony

Witnesses:
John Speed, John Ballard — /s/
Joseph Dobson

Will dated 6 July 1759 — Recorded 7 Aug. 1759

AVORIT, Thomas (Averett) — Will Book 1, Page 265

NAMES: Mentions mother, but not by name
Sister - Mary Avorit
Brother - Mathew Avorit
Brother - Henry Avorit

Makes bequest to sister Mary, but if she dies without heirs to go to brother Mathew.

Leaves personal property to mother

Executors: Friends Thomas Moore and John Potter

Witnesses:
Thomas Moore — /s/ Thomas (X) Avorit
Edward (X) Hogan

Will dated 12 March 1759 — Recorded 7 Aug. 1759

BACON, John — Will Book 1, Page 267

Inventory and appraisal of the estate of John Bacon made by John Potter, Francis Bracey (Bressie) and Edward Lewis - value 540 pounds 6 pence - returned to Court.

Recorded 4 Sept. 1759

WILLIAMSON, Thomas — Will Book 1, Page 270

An account current of the estate of Thos Williamson, deceased, returned to Court by Joseph Williams, Exec. Approved 5 Sept. 1759 by Thomas Bouldin and James Taylor, Commissioners.

Recorded 5, Sept.1759

COLBREATH, John — Will Book 1, Page 273

Inventory and appraisal of the estate of John Colbreath deceased, made by Owen Franklin, Jacob Royster and William Royster - no total given - returned to Court by Daniel McNeil, Executor, 22 Sept. 1759.

Recorded 2 Oct. 1759

RUTHERFORD, James — Will Book 1, Page 274

In obedience to an order of the Court, we Christopher Parsons, John Griffith and William Caldwell have appraised the personal estate of James Rutherford, deceased, - value 114 pounds 5 shillings ½ pence.
Returned to Court by William Rutherford, administrator.

Recorded 6 Nov. 1759

WRIGHT, John — Will Book 1, Page 277

An account current of the estate of John Wright, deceased, from 31 July 1755 to 4 July 1759, returned to Court by John Speed, administrator.
Account examined by Henry Delony, Amos Timms, Junr. and Dennis Larke, Commissioners, 24 Nov. 1759.

Recorded 4 Dec. 1759

AUSTIN, Richard — Will Book 1, Page 280

NAMES: Wife - mentioned in will but not by name.
Son - Thomas Austin
Son - Euziah Austin

Plantation left to wife during her life or widowhood, and also moveable estate, then to be divided equally "amongst my children", only the two youngest to have 2 pounds 10 shillings more than the others.

Elizabeth Vernon - 200 acres of land on south side of Terry's Run adjoining Cannon.
Sarah Joice - 200 acres of land on south side of Terry's Run adjoining Elizabeth Vernon.
Samuel David - 130 acres adjoining the plantation he now lives on.
Thomas John - 208 acres including the plantation he now lives on.

Peron Alday - 211 acres of land adjoining Thomas John

David Rice - of Hanover County - a certain parcel of land adjoining Samuel David and at the head of Sandy Creek

Estate to be kept together and not appraised. No bond to be required of the executors.

Executors: Capt. Charles Anderson and James Anderson of Cumberland County, and Joseph Morton (of Lunenburg County ?)

Witnesses:
Nathan Austin
George Caldwell
Mager (M) Washington

/s/ Rich[d] Austin

Will dated 31 March 1759 — Recorded 4 Dec. 1759

James Anderson and Joseph Morton qualified as executors

ASHWORTH, Jonathon — Will Book 1, Page 282

NAMES: Wife - not named in will and evidently deceased
Son - John Ashworth - 200 acres of land
Son - Samuel Ashworth - 300 acres of land
Son - Isaac Ashworth - 300 acres of land
Grandson - Jonathon Ashworth - 100 acres of land
Granddaughter - Elizabeth Bruce - 100 acres of land

If Elizabeth Bruce dies without heirs, land to go to my three sons John, Samuel and Isaac Ashworth.

Sons live on land bequeathed to them.

Land being a part of a patent of 1875 acres in Lunenburg County, and laid off by Sherwood Walton (Surveyor).

Executor: Son John Ashworth

Witnesses:
None recorded

/s/ Jonathon Ashworth

Dated 6 Nov. 1759 — Recorded 6 Nov. 1759

Note: The foregoing was apparently a Deed of Gift rather than the WILL of Jonathon Ashworth, but was recorded in Will Book 1. This document has the following notation under it.

Exhibited in Court by Jonathon Ashworth and acknowledged as his act. Proved at Court 6 Nov. 1759

McCLANAHAN, John — Will Book 1, Page 284

NAMES: Wife - mentioned in will but not by name
(Note: Frances McClanahan qualified as one of the executors)
Mentions two eldest sons but not by name.

To my two eldest sons my whole land and each of them to pay my son John McClanahan 20 pounds when he is of the age of 21 years.

My son William McClanahan, when he comes to age 21 years, to give my brother James McClanahan a firm deed for 150 acres of land where he did live.

My wife to the benefits of the plantation during the time she remains my widow.

After payment of my debts, and my wife gets her third, the remainder of my movable property, except three wagon horses which are to be kept for use on the plantation, to be equally divided among my daughters (not named).

Executors: William Snodgrass, my wife, and my son William McClanahan when he comes of age.

Witnesses:
Robert Rolan(d)
John (X) Boyd — /s/ John McClanahan
James Rutherford

Will dated 8 Oct. 1758 — Recorded 6 Nov. 1759

William Snodgrass and Frances McClanahan qualified on the estate with Josiah Snodgrass and Mathew Shiding ? their securities.

Notation: William McClanahan can join in probate later when he comes of age.

SMITH, Richard — Will Book 1, Page 286

NAMES: Wife - Agnes Smith
Son - Abraham Smith - the plantation whereon he now lives in the County of Dinwiddie containing 300 acres. Also one slave in the consideration of a sum of money he has paid to Mr. Boding, Merchant in London.
Son - Peter Smith
Son - Benjamin Smith

I lend use of my plantation to my wife for life, and after her decease to be divided betwen my two sons Peter and Benjamin.

Daughter - Joana Craig
Daughter - Agnes May
Son - Richard Smith
Daughter - Ann Hightower
Daughter - Temperance Booth
Daughter - Sarah Mayes
Daughter - Martha March
Daughter - Mary Booth
Daughter - Ann Smith
Daughter - Lucy Smith

Makes bequest of personal property to each named.

I lend to my wife Agnes Smith the use of my estate both real and personal for life.
To son Peter Smith, after his mother's decease, one slave.
To son Benjamin Smith, after his mother's decease, one slave.

After my wife's death, all personal property not before bequeathed to go to sons Peter and Benjamin.

Executors: Brother Abram Cocke and sons Abram and Peter Smith.

Witnesses: Abram Cocke
Peter Cocke
Abra Cocke, Junr.
Stephen Cocke

/s/ Richd Smith

Will dated 6 July 1757 — Recorded 5 Feb. 1760

Peter Smith qualified as executor with Gray Briggs, Gent., his security.

EASLEY, Thomas — Will Book 1, Page 288

Inventory and appraisal of the estate of Thomas Easley, deceased, made by Francis Mann, John East and John Barksdale - value 199 pounds 3 shillings 10½ pence - returned to Court by Matw Watson.

Recorded 5 Feb. 1760

EMBRY, William — Will Book 1, Page 290

NAMES: Wife - Elizabeth Embry
To wife Elizabeth all of my estate, real and personal, during widowhood but if she marries I lend her a child's part for life.
Son - William Embry - part of the plantation whereon I live.
Son - Henry Embry - all land on the east side of Reedy Branch.
Mentions an unborn child - if a boy - all of the rest of my lands (in Lunenburg County), but if not a boy lands to be divided between sons Henry and William.

If unborn child is a boy, I give all of my lands in Bedford County to them, but if not a boy then lands to be divided between sons William and Henry.
Daughter - Ermin Embry - slave
Daughter - Martha Embry - slave
To Elisha Brooks that part of 119 acres which lies on the south side of the south fork of branch that divides our land.

Abraham Cocke, or his heirs, shall make a good deed to William Jeter for all that land which Thomas Stith laid off for William Jeter being the land I bought of Abraham Cocke. Cocke to make title to the other lands I have bought from him.

If any son dies without heirs, the other son or sons to inherit his part.

Executors: David Garland, John Ragsdale and Thomas Edwards

Witnesses: Lazarus Williams
William Hawkins
Wm Borum
John Childress

/s/ Wm Embry

Codicil:

I left out three tracts of land on Flatrock Creek, Beaver Pond and branches thereof formerly granted to Richard Talliaferro and since then conveyed to testator; and since that conveyance the testator did covenant with and agree to sell to David Gentry, French Haggard, William Allin and James Chiswell all of this land which they agreed to divide.

Dated 7 May 1759 /s/ Wm Embry

Will dated 6 May 1759 — — Recorded 5 Feb. 1760

David Garland and John Ragsdale qualified on estate with Thomas Tabb and John Jenings their securities.

CRENSHAW, Joseph — Will Book 1, Page 292

Account current of the estate of Jos. Crenshaw, deceased, returned to Court by Thos. and Gideon Crenshaw, executors.

Approved by Richd Witton and Jos. Williams, Commissioners.

Recorded 9 Feb. 1760

COCKE, James — Will Book 1, Page 295

Account current of the estate of Mr. James Cocke, deceased, from 7 March 1757 to 1 Oct. 1759, returned by John James Dupuy, exec.

Approved 1 Oct. 1759 by Jas Taylor, Thomas Bouldin and Thomas Bedford, Comm.

Recorded 2 Oct. 1759

HUEY, Humphrey — Will Book 1, Page 303

I leave to my wife Hannah Huey my whole estate both real and personal to be at her own disposal.

Executor: Wife Hannah Huey

Witnesses: Samuel Bizwell
Robert Bizwell
Becky Bizwell

/s/ Humphrey Huey

The executrix Hannah Huey relinguished the execution of the will, and Theophilus Feild, Junr., qualified with the will annexed with Clement Read his security.

Will dated 16 Oct. 1756 Recorded 1 July 1760

WILLIS, Edward Will Book 1, Page 305

NAMES: Wife - Isbella Willis
Son - William Willis - my land on Sandy Creek containing 400 acres.
Daughter - Susanna Willis - slaves
Daughter - Rachel Willis
Mentions unborn child
Bequest - To wife negro, and at her death to go to son William, daughter Rachel and unborn child.
To wife all movable goods during her widowhood, but if she marries then to be divided between three children above.
I desire that children be educated.

Executors: Nicholas Mealer and David Halliburton

Witnesses:
Stephen Willis
James (X) Fleger
Nevill Buchanan

/s/ Edward Willis

Will dated 1760 Recorded 2 Dec. 1760

AUSTIN, John Will Book 1, Page 308

John Austin of the Parish of Cornwall, County of Lunenburg.

NAMES: Wife - Hannah Austin
Son - John Austin
Son - Valentine Austin - 400 acres on Leatherwood Creek in Halifax County.
Son - Stephen Austin - 370 acres on Sandy River in Halifax County
Son - Richard Austin
Son - Joseph Austin
To wife Hannah during her natural life plantation at head of Sandy River in Halifax County, and at her death to son Richard Austin
To wife Hannah all of the rest of my estate, both real and personal, for life and then to son Joseph Austin.
Whereas my sons Joseph, Richard and Stephen are not married, if either dies unmarried his part to go the others.

Executors: Wife Hannah and son Richard Austin

Witnesses:
George Carrington — /s/ John Austin
Isham Talbot
Thomas Read

Will dated 29 Sept. 1758 — Recorded 5 Feb. 1760

Hannah Austin relinguished her right of execution and Richard Austin qualified with Paul Carrington and Clement Read, Junr., his securities.

GRAHAM, Francis — Will Book 1, Page 310

NAMES: Wife - mentioned in will but not by name
Wife to have one-third of estate
Son - David Graham
Son - William Graham
Son - Francis Graham
Bequest: to three sons 120 pounds money to be equally divided for their schooling and maintenance.
Daughter - Jean Graham - my bay mare
Daughter - Martha Graham - mare colt

After payment of debts, balance of the estate to be divided between my four daughters Mary Graham, Jean Graham, Ann Graham and Martha Graham.

When Elisha White pays my executors 210 pounds, they are to make him a sufficient deed for the tract of land I now live on.

When Nathan Andrews pays them 40 pounds, my executors are to make a deed to him for tract of land I sold him.

Executors: John Lawson and William Lawson
Witnesses:
James Rutherford — /s/ Francis Graham
Bartlett Green

Will dated 27 July 1759 — Recorded 4 Nov. 1760

PARSONS, Christopher — Will Book 1, Page 313

NAMES: Wife - mentioned in will but not by name
Son - John Parsons - bequest
Son - William Parsons - all of my land adjoining John Weatherford
Son - Christopher Parsons - all of my land adjoining John Barksdale
Son - Major Parsons - 125 acres of land adjoining William Price
Son - Thomas Parsons
Plantation whereon I now live to my wife as long as she lives and then to son Thomas Parsons
Daughter - Agnes Parsons - furniture, etc.

My sons are to give to my daughter Agnes Parsons a cow and calf and 24 pounds money when she is age 16 years.

All of the remainder of my estate to be divided between my four sons. Each son to take his part when he comes of age.

Eldest son William Parsons to have charge of my children, and have care of their parts.

Executors: John Barksdale, Robert Weakley and Major Weatherford

Witnesses:
Thomas Paulet
William (S) Parsons
John (I) Weatherford

/s/ Christopher (S) Parsons

Will dated 6 March 1760 — Recorded 4 Nov. 1760

SANDERS, Francis (Saunders) — Will Book 1, Page 315

NAMES: Wife - mentioned in will but not by name
Children - mentioned in will but not named
Estate left to wife for life and then equally divided among my children.

Executors: Friends Richard Swepson and Thomas Carlton

Witnesses:
John Jeffries
Thomas Farguson

/s/ Francis Saunders

Will dated 13 Nov. 1760 — Recorded 2 Dec. 1760

WAGSTAFF, Francis — Will Book 1, Page 317

NAMES: Wife - Judith Wagstaff
Daughter - Elizabeth Mainard (Maynard)
Son-in-law - Nicholas Mainard (Maynard)
Bequest: To wife Judith land and plantation where I now live, together with seven negroes for life.
Bequest: To wife all movable estate, crop of tobacco, debts due to me, tobacco and cattle belonging to me in Albemarle County.
Bequest: To son-in-law Nicholas Maynard and Elizabeth Maynard land on Island Creek, together with three negroes to him and my daughter Elizabeth Maynard for her natural life.

After the death of my wife and daughter all negroes to be divided equally among my grandchildren.

Grandson - John Mainard (Maynard) - eldest
Grandson - William Mainard (Maynard)
I give to my grandsons John and William Mainard all my tract of land I now live on containing 490 acres.

If my grandsons have no heirs and Elizabeth Mainard has no more children, then my estate to go to the eldest sons of my nephew Barzil (Bazel) Wagstaff.

If they have no heirs, then the negroes left to my wife and daughter to go to my nephews, William Perkins, John Gomer, Francis Steed, John Holman and (niece) Mary Hutcherson.

If my wife dies before my grandson John Mainard shall come to lawful age, she shall appoint a guardian to look after his property.

Son-in-law Nicholas Mainard to have the stock in Albemarle County.

Executor: Wife Judith Wagstaff
Witnesses:
John Mayes /s/ Francis Wagstaff
Richard Palmer
Mathew Mayes

Will dated 14 March 1758 — Recorded 5 Aug. 1760

NORVELL, Hugh Will Book 1, Page 320

NAMES: Wife - Mary Norvell
Daughter - Elizabeth Sandefer - furniture
Daughter - Mary Norvell
Son - Thomas Norvell - plantation where I live containing 333 acres.
All rest of my estate to wife Mary for life, and then to be sold and money divided among the rest of my children.
Mentions five children but does not name others
Executor: Son Thomas Norvell
Witnesses:
William Ballard /s/ Hugh Norvell
Adam Thomson
James Smith

Will dated 20 Oct. 1759 Recorded 6 May 1760

Thomas Norvell qualified on the estate with Henry Delony, Gent., and James Coleman his securities.

McCLANAHAN, James Will Book 1, Page 322

NAMES: Brother - John McClanahan
Cousin - John McClanahan, son of my brother John
If my cousin John McClanahan dies before he comes to age then to his brother Alexander McClanahan
Brother-in-law - William Snodgrass
Sister-in-law - Frances McClanahan, widow of my brother John McClanahan
Brother - David McClanahan

Cousin - William McClanahan, son of my brother David McClanahan
Cousin - Samuel McClanahan, son of my brother David McClanahan
Bequests made to all named.

Executor: Brother-in-law William Snodgrass

Witnesses:
Robert Weakley /s/ James (Ø) McClanahan
James Rutherford

Will dated 27 Oct. 1758 Recorded 7 July 1761

FUQUA, William Will Book 1, Page 323

NAMES: Wife - Elizabeth Fuqua
To wife Elizabeth the plantation whereon I now live for her natural life.
Son - Samuel Fuqua
Son - Joseph Fuqua
After death of my wife, lands left to her to be divided between sons Samuel and Joseph Fuqua.
Son - Moses Fuqua all my tract of land in Bedford County at Sturgeon town.
Son - William Fuqua all my tract of land on the Dan River where William Robinson now lives.
Son - John Fuqua - slaves
Daughter - Sarah Ward - slaves
Bequest - To wife slaves and personal property to be divided at her death among all children.

Executors: Wife Elizabeth and sons John and Joseph Fuqua

Witnesses:
Thomas Watkins /s/ William (Ø) Fuqua
Thomas (X) Baughan
John Baughan Joseph East
Jam[s] Anderson

Will dated 11 Dec. 1760 Recorded 3 March 1761

JOHNSTON, James Will Book 1, Page 326

NAMES: Wife - mentioned in will but not by name
Son - John Johnston
Son - James Johnston
Bequest of personal property to two sons
Son - Samuel Johnston
Daughter - Ann Johnston
Daughter - Esther Johnston
Mentions his seven children but does not name other children
Son John to pay each child his part as he or she comes of age.

Executor to collect all money due me in this Colony or in the Province of Pennsylvania whether by bond, bill or account. Said money to be divided equally between my wife and <u>seven</u> children.

Samuel, Ann and Esther to be schooled out of my estate without diminishing any part of their legacy.

Executor: Son John Johnston

Witnesses:

David Caldwell — /s/ James Johnston

Wm Caldwell

David Logan, Senr.

Will dated 22 Aug. 1760 — Recorded 3 March 1761

CHILDERS, Henry — Will Book 1, Page 328

NAMES: Wife - Mary Childers

To wife Mary plantation whereon I now live containing 200 acres of land. Also movable property for life or widowhood.

Son - John Childers - personal property

Son - Henry Childers - plantation containing 200 acres as laid off to my wife and then to him.

Son - Thomas Childers - 200 acres of land being part of my plantation.

If my wife marries again, then all movable estate left to her to be equally divided among my many children, namely, John, Lucresha, Phebia, Anne, Henry, Thomas, Millicent, Mary, Godfrey, Sarah and David Childers.

Executor: Friend Paul Carrington

Witnesses:

William Goen — /s/ Henry Childers

Thos Rutledge

William (M) Mullings

Will dated 1 Dec. 1760 — Recorded 3 March 1761

CALDWELL, William — Will Book 1, Page 329

NAMES: Wife - Rebeccah Caldwell

Son - John Caldwell

Other children mentioned but not by name.

Executors to inventory and sell enough of my personal estate to pay debts.

Executors to sell all my lands except that part of the plantation where I now live lying on the south side of Great Louse Creek, including mill and houses.

My wife to have this plantation and slave to support children until son John arrives at age 21 years.

Each of my children to have a child's part

of my personal estate after debts are paid.
Children may be bound out to learn a trade if my executors think fit to do so.

Executors: Brothers David and Robert Caldwell

Witnesses:
John Fulton /s/ Wm Caldwell
James Cunningham
William (y) McAllin

Will dated 9 Jan. 1758

Codicil 17 Feb. 1761 - I do hereby ratify and confirm the whole of the within will.

Witnesses:
Richard Dudgeon
Robt. Mitchell /s/ Wm Caldwell
James Cunningham

Names wife Rebeccah as one of executors.

Recorded 7 April 1761

HOLMES, Joseph — Will Book 1, Page 332

NAMES: Wife - mentioned in will but not by name
Brother - John Holmes
Nephew - Thomas Holmes, son of my brother John Holmes.
Daughter-in-law - Anne Turner - 2 sheep
Son-in-law - Edmond Turner - 2 sheep
Bequest: - To wife one-third part of estate, real and personal.
Remainder of estate to Thomas Holmes, son of my brother John Holmes.

Executor: Cousin (nephew) Thomas Holmes

Witnesses:
William Baughan /s/ Thomas (xxx) Holmes
Thomas Baughan
Joseph Hunt William (W) Glass

Will dated 17 Dec. 1761 — Recorded 2 Feb. 1762

Thomas Holmes, executor named, produced the will in Court.

Rosemond Holmes, widow and relict by deed dated 1 Feb. 1762, renounced all benefit and advantage she might have by any legacy bequeathed to her in the will.

HOLMES, Rosemond — Will Book 1, Page 333

To the Worshipful Court of Lunenburg County:

This Deed Witnesseth, that a considerable part of the estate that Joseph Holmes died possessed of came by his marriage with me, and as he has not made sufficient provision in his will for my support, he having no children, I rely on the provision the law has made for relief of the distressed and I renounce the provisions of the will.

Witnesses:
Joseph Hunt — /s/ Rosemond (R) Holmes
John Fuqua
Thomas Holmes

Dated 1 day of Feb. 1762 — Recorded 2 Feb. 1762

WELLS, George — Will Book 1, Page 334

NAMES: Wife - mentioned in will but not by name
Son - Elijah Wells
Son - Abner Wells
Land where I now live to be equally divided between my sons Elijah and Abner Wells
Daughter - Susanna Wells - personal property
My wife to have remainder of my estate for life, and then to be divided among my children, Elijah, Hannah, Ann, Susanna and Abner Wells.

Executors: Elijah Wells and Frederick Nance

Witnesses:
Geo. Walton — /s/ George Wells
Barnaby (B) Wells
Edward (X) Hayley

Will dated 2 Sept. 1761 — Recorded 6 Oct. 1761

SMITHSON, John — Will Book 1, Page 336

NAMES: Wife - mentioned in will but not by name
To my wife all of my estate, goods and chattels, all personal estate and whatsoever I own.

Executor: Wife (name not stated)

Witnesses:
Robt. Breedlove — /s/ John (J) Smithson
Isbel Johnson Breedlove
Kindness (X) Shorter

Will dated 6 April 1760 — Recorded 1 Dec. 1761

COCKE, James — Will Book 1, Page 336

NAMES: Brother - William Cocke
To brother William Cocke the plantation where I now live except 15 acres at the lower end.
Friend - Thomas Anderson - gives him 15 acres
Mentions mother but not by name
Sister - Susannah Coleman - negro
Sister - Anne Cocke - negro

Sister - Mary Anderson - negro
Sister - Martha Cocke - negro
To brother William Cocke remainder of my estate, and he to pay my debts and give to my mother 50 pounds to be disposed of by her as she thinks fit.

Executors: Brother William Cocke and friend Edmund Taylor

Witnesses:
Richard Hall
Thos Bracey
John Lynch

/s/ James Cocke

Will dated 1 Feb. 1761 — Recorded 1 Dec. 1761

SEAT, Josiah — Will Book 1, Page 338

NAMES: Wife - not named in will and deceased
Son - Robert Seat
To son Robert Seat all my land on Blue Wing Creek in Halifax County.
Daughter - Mary Seat - land on which I now live but if she dies without heirs land to go to son Robert Seat
Daughter - Margaret Gold - remainder of this tract of land
Daughter - Sarah Seat
Daughter - Elizabeth Seat
To daughters Sarah and Elizabeth my land on upper side of Buffalo Creek
After payment of debts, all of the rest of my estate to be divided among all of my children.

Executor: Jacob Royster

Witnesses:
Richard Jones
Robert Jones
John (X) Bray

/s/ Josiah Seat

Will dated 20 June 1760 — Recorded 1 Dec. 1761

CHAMBLISS, Nathaniel — Will Book 1, Page 339

NAMES: Wife - Mary Chambliss
Plantation to wife Mary for life or widowhood. Personal property.
Son - John Chambliss - 100 acres and personal property
Son - Nathaniel Chambliss - remainder of my land and personal property
At death of wife, personal property left her to be divided equally between my younger children, Henry, Molly and William Chambliss
Son John to pay my wife and children 10 pounds

Executor: Wife Mary Chambliss

Witnesses:
John Howell /s/ Nathaniel (X) Chambliss
John Parker
Jeremiah (T) Mize

Will dated Recorded 1 Dec. 1761

Mary Chambliss, widow and relict, refused to qualify as executrix, and renounced all benefit by any bequest in will.

John Chambliss qualified as administrator with the will annexed with John Parker his security.

SANDFORD, John Will Book 1, Page 340

NAMES: Wife - Frances Sandford
Daughter - Elizabeth Sandford
Daughter - Frances Sandford
Mentions unborn child
Provides for sale of land "I live on". One-third money received for land to go to wife.
Provides for sale of as much personal property as may be necessary to pay debts.
Balance of money from sale of land to be used to buy negroes which with their increase are to be equally divided for my daughters Elizabeth and Sarah Sandford as they shall marry or come of age.

If unborn child lives, then one-fourth of estate to go to wife and each child instead of one-third.

Executors: Friend John Ragsdale and wife Frances Sandford

Witnesses:
David Garland Jn° (S) Sanford
Edward (I) Jackson
Elizabeth (X) Ballard

Will dated 30 March 1762 Recorded 4 May 1762

WARD, Richard Will Book 1, Page 341

NAMES: Wife - Mary Ward
Son - Benjamin Ward - 120 acres in County of Cumberland adjoining James Brown, Jonas Reanuls, Valentine Colley
To wife Mary 350 acres of land in Lunenburg County, six slaves and personal property.
Daughter - Tahpenah Ward

Mentions unborn child, and bequeaths to the unborn child 150 acres in Chesterfield County between the road and the river adjoining Eliza Gay and Seth Ward.

Bequeaths to unborn child, also, 1010 acres of land in Cumberland County between Angola Creek and Appomattox River, all of the land I now enjoy in Lunenburg County, all negroes I have in Cumberland and Lunenburg Counties and six negroes lent to my wife after her death.

Executors: Friend Seth Ward and Perrin Alday

Witnesses:
Abra. Martin
Neah (?) Frank
Joshua Wharton

/s/ Richard Ward

Will dated 17 Nov. 1759 — Recorded 2 July 1762

Perrin Alday qualified as executor with Alexander Joyce Thomas Joyce, John Pettus, Dudley Barksdale, Francis Cook, William Cook and John Rice as his securities.

McDANIEL, Terrence — Will Book 1, Page 343

NAMES: Wife - not named in will and evidently deceased
Son - Elisha McDaniel
Bequest to son Elisha my tract of land on Straightstone Creek in Halifax County and all personal property.
Son Elisha to be schooled five years from age nine years to 14 years, and then to be bound out to learn a trade.
I desire that my personal estate be appraised and sold publicly as soon after my death as possible.
If my son Elisha dies without heir, or heirs, I desire that my property go to Susanna Maxey, daughter of Radford and Elizabeth Maxey.

Executor: Friend Radford Maxey

Witnesses:
William Black
William Sims
Mary Dudgeon

/s/ Terrehs (T) McDaniel

Will dated 9 April 1762 — Recorded 4 May 1762

Radford Maxey qualified as executor with Paul Carrington his security.

TRAYLOR, William — Will Book 1, Page 345

Names: Wife - Mary Traylor
Son - Joel Traylor - given horse at age 21
Son - William Traylor - given land and plantation where I now live.
Daughter - Mary Hood - one shilling Sterling
Daughter - Ann Moore - one shilling Sterling
If I have any right to the land land called the "Fleets", it is to be divided equally between my wife Mary Traylor and my children, Joel, William, Isabella, Agnes and Elizabeth Traylor.

Bequeathed to wife Mary Traylor all remainder of estate during her life to maintain my younger children, and then to be divided between my three younger daughters. (Isabella, Agnes and Elizabeth Traylor ?)

Executor: Wife Mary Traylor

Witnesses:

Jno Hobson /s/ William (Ø) Traylor

David Darden

William Clift

Will dated 18 Sept. 1761 Recorded 2 Feb. 1762

Mary Traylor qualified as executrix with John Hobson her security.

DYER, Robert Will Book 1, Page 346

NAMES: Wife - Elizabeth Dyer

Mentions father and mother, but not by name

Daughter - Martha Dyer

To my late daughter - not named

Makes bequests of slaves to each.

Executors: Father Robert Dyer and George Phillips

Witnesses:

Philemon Payne /s/ Robt Dyer R/

Charles Hamlin, Junr.

Reps. Jones

Will dated 18 March 1761 Recorded 2 March 1762

POLLARD, William Will Book 1, Page 347

NAMES: Wife - Agnes Pollard

Daughter - Agnes Hopkins - gives slave and horse

Son - Benjamin Pollard - gives three slaves and plantation "where I now live".

All rest of estate to wife Agnes Pollard, but son Benjamin Pollard to support her.

Mentions law suit in regard to his father's estate in Louisa County. If estate is recovered to be divided among all of my children (not named), and each is to pay their part of the cost of the suit.

Executors: Son Benjamin Pollard and William Landrum

Witnesses:

David Hopkins /s/ Wm Pollard

Mat Sims, Junr.

Thos (X) Hill

Will dated 2 March 1761 Recorded 1 Sept. 1761

Benjamin Pollard and William Landrum qualified as the executors with David Hopkins, John Hobson and John White their securities.

BRESSIE, Francis — Will Book 1, Page 348

NAMES: Wife - Elizabeth Bressie
Grandson - William Bressie - gives 400 acres of land
Son - Thomas Bressie ?
Son - John Bressie ?
Daughter - Elizabeth Bressie ?
I have already given them .. (their share) .... (will mutilated)
To my wife all (rest of) my estate, both real and personal, to dispose of as she pleases.
My wife to receive .... and to pay all just debts.

Executor: Wife (not named by name)

Witnesses:
Irby Bressie
Nath. Bacon
Spencer Pescud

/s/ Fran^s Bressie

Will dated 16 Jan. 1761 — Recorded 2 March 1762

Elizabeth Bressie qualified as executrix with Thomas Bressie and Thomas ________ (mutilated) her securities.

LANGLEY, Margaret — Will Book 1, Page 349

NAMES: Husband - not mentioned
(Widow of John Langley ?)
Daughter - Elizabeth Hyde - makes specific bequest, and gives residue of estate to her.
Son - Thomas Langley - 12 pounds to be raised out of estate

Executors: Friends John Hyde and Thomas Hawkins

Witnesses:
Isaac Mitchell
Joseph Akin
Reuben ______ (mutilated)

/s/ (mutilated)

Will dated (mutilated) Feb. 1756 — Recorded (mutilated)

Note: Pages 348 and 349 mutilated. The will of Francis Bressie was proved by witnesses and ordered recorded 2 March 1762, but Elizabeth Bressie did not qualify until 2 May 1762.

Presumedly, the will of Margaret Langley was proved and recorded 2 May 1762.

NANCE, John | Will Book 2, Page 1

NAMES: Wife - not named in will and deceased
Son - John Nance - gives 1 shilling Sterling
Son - Thomas Nance - gives 1 shilling Sterling
Son - Richard Nance - gives 1 shilling Sterling
Son - William Nance - gives 1 shilling Sterling
Son - Frederick Nance - gives him "the land and plantation whereon I now live" (but subject to right of daughters below)
Daughter - Sarah Nance - gives 1 shilling Sterling.
Daughter - Jane Nance - gives 1 shilling Sterling.
Daughter - Phebe Nance - gives 1 shilling Sterling.
Daughter - Susannah Nance - gives 1 shilling Sterling
Daughter - Elizabeth Nance)
Daughter - Molly Nance) gives to them the "land and plantation" for their use together with slave named Jack while they remain unmarried, then to son Frederick.

All of the rest of estate, after payment of debts and legacies, to be divided equally between daughters Elizabeth and Molly Nance.

Executor: Son Thomas Nance

Witnesses:
Geo. Walton | /s/ John Nance
Hezekiah Jackson
Benj. Ship

Will dated 28 Feb. 1761 | Recorded 3 Aug. 1762

EDMONDSON, Thomas | Will Book 2, Page 3

NAMES: Wife - Grissell Edmondson
Bequest - To wife Grissell for her natural life my now dwelling plantation will all of my personal estate.
Youngest son - Benjamin Edmondson
Bequest - The plantation given my wife containing 100 acres at her death

All of the rest of may lands to be equally divided among all of my sons (not named) as they come of age.

Personal estate, at death of my wife, to be divided among my daughters (not named).

Executors: My wife and Randall Bracey

Witnesses:
Bryant (X) Creedle | /s/ Thomas Edmondson
Peter (X) Parrish
Thomas (T) Adams

Will dated 21 May 1755 Recorded 5 Aug. 1760

Randall Bracey qualified as executor with Thomas Adams his security. Grissell Edmondson given liberty to join in qualification if she thinks fit to do so.

BARKLEY, James (Bartley) Will Book 2, Page 5

NAMES: Wife - mentioned in will but not by name
(wife named as executor but not by name - Jean Barkley qualified on estate)
Daughter - Ginny Barkley
Barkley Grayer - connection not stated - bequeaths him 5 pounds in money
Bequest - To daughter Ginny sorrel horse, furniture and other property as her mother thinks fit.
Smith's tools to be sold to pay debts.
Remainder of estate to wife, and at her decease, to be disposed of as she thinks proper.
Executor: Wife (not named)
Witnesses:
Phill Russell /s/ James (B) Bartley
Drury Moore
John Callihan
Will dated 12 May 1761 Recorded 1 June 1762

Jean Barkley qualified as executrix with Joseph Green and Thomas Leveritt her securities.

CUNNINGHAM, Andrew Will Book 2, Page 6

NAMES: Wife - Jean Cunningham
Daughter - Jean Cunningham
Daughter - Elizabeth Cunningham
Oldest Daughter - Mary George
Granddaughter - Margaret George - gives her six sheep and 5 pounds in money.
Bequest to granddaughter to be taken out of the estate before any division.
Daughter Mary George has been given her share of my estate.
Estate to be divided - one-third to wife, one-third to daughter Jean and one-third to daughter Elizabeth.
Wife Jean to enjoy her third for life or widowhood, and then to be equally divided between two daughters.
Executors can adjust and make a division of land.
Executors: James McMachen and John Cunningham

Witnesses:
Matthew Cunningham /s/ Andrew (S) Cunningham
James Daughtery
William Cunningham

Will dated 23 Sept. 1760 Recorded 5 May 1761

Note: James McMachen and John Cunningham both of Prince Edward County. Executors qualified with John Scott and William Cunningham their securities.

GREEN, Henry Will Book 2, Page 8

NAMES: Wife - mentioned in will but not by name.
Henry Jackson - son of William Jackson
John Owen - son of Joseph Owen

Gives to John Owen and Henry Jackson "the land where I now live", to be divided eqaally between them when they come of age, but wife to have use of land during her widowhood.

Bequests: To John Owen my mare Silver and my guh.

To Darcus Jackson, my sister, cow and calf and hogs.

To my wife the rest of my goods and chattels.

Executors: William Sizemore and John Green
Witnesses:
George Moore /s/ Henry Green
Stephen Green
Frederick Green

Will dated 23 Feb. 1761 Recorded 5 May 1761

Executors qualified with Jacob Royster and Richard Yancey their securities.

PALMER, Parmenas Will Book 2, Page 9

NAMES: Wife - Mary Ann Palmer
Bequest: To wife my land and plantation where I now live for life and then to my son Joshua Palmer

Son - Thomas Palmer - gives him a survey of land on Allen's Creek

After debts are paid, remainder of estate to be equally divided between my wife Mary Ann, sons William Palmer, Thomas Palmer and Joshua Palmer, and (daughters) Martha Palmer, Sarah Palmer and Winifred Palmer

Executors: Wife Mary Ann Palmer, brother William Palmer and son William Palmer
Witnesses:
None recorded /s/ (will not signed)

Will dated 24 Aug. 1761 Recorded 6 Oct. 1761

Will accepted as a nuncupative will proven by the oaths of Christopher Hudson and Rebecca Palmer and ordered to be recorded.

WILES, Stephen Will Book 2, Page 10

NAMES: Wife - Mary Wiles
Bequests: Furniture and a bay mare
The land whereon I now live containing 200 acres, my entry (for land) on the Great branch of Aarons Creek, with all of the rest of my estate, both movable and immovable, to be sold by my executors, and after payment of debts remain- to be given to my wife Mary Wiles.
The tract of land at the mouth of Buffalo Creek is patented in my name and that of Lewis Dupree.
My executors are to make a deed to Robert Wiles for the upper half of said tract, and to Joseph Dupree for the other half.
To Thomas Wiles all right and title to the land which my father left to me on the south side of the Roanoke River.
Executors: Thomas Wiles and Joseph Dupree
Witnesses: Nevil Buckannon, Robert Wiles, Luke Wiles and Aaron Pinson
Will dated 5 May 1762 Recorded 1 June 1762

Joseph Dupree renounced the execution of the will and Thomas Wiles qualified as executor with Thomas Dupree his security.

PATTERSON, Erwin Will Book 2, Page 11

NAMES: Wife - Elenora Patterson
Daughter - Margaret Patterson
Mentions unborn child
Debts to be paid out of money arising from my estate
Bequests - To Erwin Wood, son of John Wood, a tract of land in Augusta County containing 40 acres on south side of West Roanoke River, being part of a larger tract formerly belonging to John Thomas of said county.
John Mills of Lunenburg County to execute a deed to Israel Christian of Augusta County for a tract of land containing 80 acres in Augusta County adjoining the tract of land where I formerly lived called Stone House.
To my three friends, John Mills, Thomas

Rodgers and James Patterson, 20 pounds Virginia Money each to be raised out of my estate.

My executors to pay to John Crawley 10 pounds, a new suit of clothes and a man's saddle.

To my wife, Elenora Patterson, 200 pounds to be raised out of my estate, horse and personal property.

To my wife, during widowhood, the use of all rents and profits from all my remaining land in Augusta County.

If my wife (and her mother) should die or marry before my daughter Margaret arrives at age 18 years, (then) Margaret is to be sole owner of land and other property in Augusta County. If my wife be with child, then the property to be divided between the two children.

My wife to live on property where they now reside, movable property to be sold and money put at interest for use of child or children.

Executors: John Mills, Thomas Rodgers and James Patterson

Witnesses: Nathaniel Patterson, Jane Mills, Mary Mills and John Wood

Will dated 11 Feb. 1761 — Recorded 5 May 1761

PHILLIPS, John — Will Book 2, Page 14

NAMES: Wife - Mary Phillips

Bequest - To wife Mary land and all of my estate after debts are paid

Son - John Phillips)
Son - Antony Phillips) Estate left to wife after her death.

If my wife is with child and it is a son, he is to share with other two sons.

Son - Robin Phillips - one shilling Sterling

Daughter - Mary Phillips - one shilling Sterling

After death of my wife, all of my estate, except land, to be divided among my daughters - Nancy Phillips and Elizabeth Phillips, if my wife is with child and she is a daughter, the child to share with other daughters.

Executor: Edward Waller

Witnesses: Thomas Sammons and Ann Waller

Will dated 29 Nov. 1760 — Recorded 4 Aug. 1761

BAILEY, Henry — Will Book 2, Page 15

NAMES: Wife - Avis Bailey

Bequest to wife - furniture, mare and saddle.

Son - William Bailey - Land and Plantation where I now live.

Such of my estate that is left after death of my wife to be divided equally among all of my children (not named)

Executor: Son William Bailey

Witnesses: Wm Turner, John (X) Wray and Matthew Turner

Will dated 28 Feb. 1761 — Recorded 5 May 1761

WIMPIE, John — Will Book 2, Page 16

NAMES: Grandson - Henry Wimpie, son of John Wimpie, Jr. and Elenor his wife.

Bequest to grandson - 183 acres of land. He is to have possession of land at age 16 years, but is to pay to his sister - Elizabeth Wimpie - the sum of 8 pounds Virginia Money when he is age 25 years.

The remainder of my estate and all accounts to go to Benjamin Atkins and his heirs.

Executor: None named in will

Witnesses: Daniel Cargill, John Lucas and Benj^{a} Atkins

Will dated 24 Sept. 1761 — Recorded 6 July 1762

Note: No record in will book in regard to administrator following recorded will

MIZE, James — Will Book 2, Page 17

NAMES: Wife - Elizabeth Mize

Son - Stephen Mize - 200 acres of land which he now lives on.

Son - William Mize - My plantation whereon I now live, and my water mill with improvements and 15 acres of land.

Grandson - Joseph Wright - Furniture after death of my wife

Son - James Mize - Furniture (to be given after death of my wife)

Wife Elizabeth - To have residue of estate, and after her death to be divided equally between James Mize, Stephen Mize, William Mize, John Wright and Thomas Wright

Since I have more than enough estate to pay my debts, I desire that estate be not appraised.

Executor: Son Stephen Mize

Witnesses: John Wright, William Mize, Thomas Wright and John Hight

Will dated 2 Feb. 1761 — Recorded 7 April 1761

FOSTER, George — Will Book 2, Page 19

NAMES: Wife - Mary Foster

Son - John Foster

Son - Josiah Foster

Daughter - Sarah Foster
Debts to be paid, negro George purchased from Matthew Flournoy to be sold.
Bequests - To wife Mary the plantation where I now live for widowhood, and after her death or remarriage land to go to son John Foster and his heirs.
- To son Josiah the tract of land purchased from Moses Hall containing 200 acres.
- To daughter Sarah the tract of land in Caroline County containing 200 acres.

Residue of my estate to be divided between my wife Mary and my three children John, Jósiah and Sarah at the discretion of my executors.
Children all under age.

Executors: Wife Mary Foster and brothers William and Josiah Foster
Witnesses: C. Read, Jr., William Hatchett and Jo. Foster.

Will dated 30 Aug. 1762 Recorded 5 Oct. 1762

Note: Executors qualified with Henry Isbell, Thomas Nance and Clem[t] Read, Jr., their securities, but George Foster is listed as George Foster, Jr. in qualification on estate.

BROWN, Israel Will Book 2, Page 21

NAMES: Wife - Ann Brown
Bequest to wife - all movable property, slaves, plantation 300 acres where I now live.
Son - Isaac Brown - Bequest to son - my still and any part of my land "not interrupting his mother".
Daughter - Lucy Cralle - Part of the tract of my Flat Rock plantation and part of the stock (on this plantation).
Son - Jacob Brown - Bequest of 300 acres of land on the south side of the North Fork of Moodys Branch.
Son - Robert Brown - Bequest of 300 acres of land on Moodys Branch.
Son - Sterwin (Sherwin ?) Brown - Bequest of 200 acres on Flat Rock Creek. (May be Stephen)
Four daughters - Sarah, Jane, Ann and Amey Brown - 20 pounds each, and after death of my wife Ann Brown to have 400 acres on north side of Flat Rock Creek.
Son - Abraham Brown - Tract of land on Beaver pon (sic) Creek.
Provides that if Isaac dies without heirs his part of land to go to Stephen Brown.

Provides that son Isaac may settle on (home) land and build a house, but his mother is not to be disturbed.
Daughters - minors and to be of age at 18 years.
Sons - minors apparently, and their land shall be at their disposal at age 18 years.

Executors: Wife Ann Brown and son Isaac Brown
Witnesses: Barnabe Noland and Thomas Trammell
Will dated 22 Aug. 1757 Recorded 5 Aug. 1760

Note: Ann Brown qualified as executrix with John Ragsdale and Phillemon Russell her securities, reserving liberty for Isaac Brown to qualify later (after coming of legal age apparently).

CUNNINGHAM, James Will Book 2, Page 26

NAMES: Wife - Jane Cunnignham
Son - John Cunningham
Son - William Cunningham
Bequests - To son John 212 acres on Rober(t)sons River, being part of a tract of land purchased of Capt. Joseph Williamson
- To son William 213 acres, being part of same tract, and slave.
Son - James Cunningham - the land and plantation whereon I now live and slaves.
Gives to sons stock and personal property.
Estate left to wife for life and then to be divided between three sons.

Executor: Wife Jane Cunningham
Witnesses: Thomas Pettus, Daniel Hay and Matthew Hay
Will dated 2 Oct. 1762 Recorded 2 Nov. 1762

JOHNSTON, Joseph * Will Book 2, Page 28

NAMES: Wife - Mary Johnson
Son - Mical Johnston - slave and stock
Son - Isaac Johnston - slave and stock
Daughter - Sarah Womack - personal property
Daughter - Mary Winningham - one shilling Sterling
Son - David Johnston - 8 shillings 8 pence which he owes me.
Daughter - Ann Wood - slave
Son - Joseph Johnson - cattle and 200 acres of land whereon he now lives.
Daughter - Susannah Hudson - cattle
Daughter - Elizabeth Johnston - personal propert
Daughter - Sisley Johnston - personal property
Lends all property, not mentioned in will, to wife Mary, but if she marries to go to daughter Charity Johnston

Daughter - Charity Johnston - to be given 100 pounds now in the hands of her mother Daughter Charity to get all property in the hand's of my wife on her death.

Executors: John Brown and Sherwood Walton
Witnesses: Isaac Johnson, Jno. Thomason and Ann Brown
Will dated 8 Jan. 1761 Recorded 3 March 1761

* Recorded as both Johnston and Johnson, but signed "Joseph Johnson".

PHILLIPS, John Will Book 2, Page 31

Inventory and appraisal of the estate of John Phillips, deceased, - nothing given - returned to Court and ordered recorded. Recorded 3 Aug. 1762

COCKE, James Will Book 2, Page 32

Appraisal of the estate of James Cocke, deceased, returned to Court by Wm Cocke - value 337 pounds 2 shillings 2 pence.

Recorded 2 Nov. 1762

PALMER, Parmenas Will Book 2, Page 33

Inventory and appraisal of the estate of Parmenas Palmer made by John Hyde, James Easter and Robt. Coleman returned to Court - value 54 pounds 2 shillings.

Recorded 3 Aug. 1762

McDANIEL, Terrence Will Book 2, Page 35

By an order of May Court 1762, we Richard Dudgeon, Isaac Vernon and Henry Tate have appraised the estate of Terrence McDaniel - no total given - returned to Court by Radford Maxey, executor.

Recorded 3 Aug. 1762

HARWOOD, George Will Book 2, Page 37

An account current of the estate of George Harwood, deceased, returned by David Caldwell and Jno. Logan, executors. To Agnes Harwood - 36 pounds 11 shillings - agreeable to the testator's will for the support of the widow and children on a tract of land on Ward's Fork. Certified by Jas. Taylor and Thos. Bedford, comm. 3 Aug 1762. Recorded 3 Aug. 1762

LITCHFIELD, Joseph Will Book 2, Page 42

Inventory of the estate of Joseph Litchfield, deceased, made under order of May Court 1760 by John Ragsdale, Peter Cocke and Benj^a Bridgforth - value 62 pounds 12 shillings 11½ pence - returned to Court and ordered recorded. Recorded 4 Nov. 1760

WRENN, Thomas Will Book 2, Page 43

Inventory and appraisal of the estate of Thomas Wrenn, deceased, made by Jo[s] Morton, Sam. Morton and Tho[s] Spencer - value 62 pounds 16 shillings - and account of sales totaling 59 pounds 2 shillings 2 pence - returned to Court by James French and ordered to be recorded.
Recorded 7 Dec. 1762

CALDWELL, William Will Book 2, Page 44

In obddience to an order of the Lunenburg County Court dated the first Tuesday of August 1761, we have met and settled the estate of William Caldwell, miller, deceased as offered to us by Thomas Daurity (sic).
/s/ James Hunt
/s/ David Caldwell

Account of which Thomas Daughtery is administrator returned and ordered to be recorded.
Recorded 2 Feb. 1762

NANCE, John Will Book 2, Page 45

Inventory and appraisal of the estate of John Nance, deceased, made by Daniel Malone, Robert Beasley and Jarril Willingham 14 August 1762 - value 58 pounds 16 shillings 3 pence - returned to Court.
Recorded 3 Sep. 1762

ROBINSON, Abraham Will Book 2, Page 47

Inventory and appraisal of the estate of Abraham Robinson made by Timothy Smith, John Wilson and Bruce Miller - value 32 pounds 3 pence - returned to Court.
Recorded 2 Feb. 1762

DANIEL, Leonard Will Book 2, Page 48

Account current of the estate of Leonard Daniel, deceased, 7 Sept. 1761, showing list of accounts to be paid by Chisley Daniel, administrator - total 163 pounds 13 shillings 8 pence.

Will Book 2, Page 49

Inventory of goods and chattels sold to discharge debts of estate (all in possession of me Chisley Daniel, administrator). Part sold 7 Sept. 1761 and part sold 29 Jan. 1762 - total 146 pounds 17 shillings 1½ pence.
Recorded 7 April 1762

BUGG, Sherwood — Will Book 2, Page 51

Inventory and appraisal of the estate of Sherwood Bugg made 31 Aug. 1761 by Sam[l] Bugg, Walter Lee and Anselm Bugg - value 15 pounds 2 shillings.

Recorded 1 June 1762

WAGSTAFF, Francis — Will Book 2, Page 51

Inventory of the estate of Francis Wagstaff, deceased, taken 1 September 1760, returned to Court by Judith Wagstaff.

Recorded 5 Nov. 1760

FARMER, George — Will Book 2, Page 52

Pursuant to an order of the Worshipful Court of Lunenburg County to us directed, we John Cargill, Daniel Cargill and Corn[s] Cargill, Junr., have appraised the estate of George Farmer, deceased - value not given.

Recorded 1 Sept. 1761

CHILDRESS, Henry (Childers) — Will Book 2, Page 53

An inventory of the estate of Henry Childress, deceased returned by Paul Carrington, exec. 1 Aug. 1761.

Recorded 6 Oct. 1761

WILES, Stephen — Will Book 2, Page 56

By order of the Lunenburg Court held October 1762, we were first sworn and then appraised all such estate of Stephen Wiles, deceased, as was brought before us on 9 Oct. 1762 - total value not given - signed by John Jones, William Royster and Edward Colbreath.

Recorded 7 Dec. 1762

FLYN, Laughlin — Will Book 2, Page 57

Pursuant to an order of Court, we have proceeded to value and appraise the estate of Laughlin Flyn, deceased.

The hole (sic) amount is 139 pounds 18 shillings 3 pence, current money of Virginia.

Given under our hands 13 Aug. 1762 - /s/ W[m] Hunt, William Harris and John Tomson

Recorded 7 Sept. 1762

AUSTIN, John — Will Book 2, Page 60

An account of the sails (sic) of the estate of John Austin, deceased made 12 March 1761 - value 47 pounds 10 shillings 6 pence.

Recorded 7 Oct. 1761

EMBRY, William, Gent. Will Book 2, Page 62

Pursuant to an order of the February Court 1760, we appraised the estate of William Embry, deceased, 19 Feb. 1761 - value 1126 pounds 6 shillings 4½ pence. /s/ William Gordon, Richard Williams and Lazarus Williams. Returned to Court and ordered recorded.

Recorded 6 May 1760

PALMER, Capt. Richard Will Book 2, Page 64

Inventory and appraisal of the estate of Capt. Richard Palmer made 15 Sept. 1761 by John Camp, Thos Moore and Thos Satterwhite - value 976 pounds 6 pence - returned to Court and ordered recorded.

Recorded 6 Oct. 1761

HUNT, Joseph Will Book 2, Page 66

Inventory of the personal estate of Joseph Hunt, deceased, taken 13 Sept. 1760 by Henry Williams, Edward Elam and Wm B. Brown - value 8 pounds 19 shillings 11 pence.

Recorded 2 Nov. 1761

GRIMES, Francis Will Book 2, Page 68

Inventory and appraisal of the estate of Francis Grimes deceased, made by John McNeese, Richard Gittens and John McDavitt - value not stated - returned to Court.

Will Book 2, Page 69

List of sales of the estate of Francis Grimes, deceased made 4 Dec. 1760, returned to Court by John Lawson and Wm Lawson, executors - total not given.

Recorded 3 March 1761

ANDREWS, Robert Will Book 2, Page 71

Inventory and appraisal of the estate of Robert Andrews deceased, made 18 Oct. 1761 by Robt. Wood and Robt Caldwell - value 73 pounds 5 shillings 9 pence.

Recorded 1 June 1762

STONE, William Will Book 2, Page 73

Inventory and appraisal of the estate of Willm Stone, deceased, made 17 Jan. 1761 by John Winn, James Pulliam and Joseph Pulliam - value 36 pounds ½ pence.

Recorded 3 March 1761

JAMES, John Will Book 2, Page 75

Inventory and appraisal of the present personal estate

of John James, deceased, made 17 May 1760 - value 9 pounds 5 shillings 6 pence - appraisers not named.

Recorded 4 Nov. 1760

PARSONS, Christopher — Will Book 2, Page 76

Inventory and appraisal of the estate of Christopher Parsons, deceased, made by Thomas Ward, Matthew Watson and Elisha White - no value given.

Recorded 3 March 1761

JOHNSON, Joseph — Will Book 2, Page 79

Pursuant to an order of the Lunenburg County Court, we, Thomas Nance, Henry Blagrave and William Chandler, have appraised the estate of Joseph Johnson, deceased, as shown us by Sherwood Walton, Exec. - value 994 pounds 12 shillings 9 pence - returned to Court 7 July 1761.

Recorded 7 July 1761

LANGFORD, John — Will Book 2, Page 84

Inventory and appraisal of the estate of John Langford made by James Dawes, Francis Bowers and Edward Jackson 7 August 1762 - value 34 pounds 9 shillings 9 pence - returned to Court and ordered recorded.

Recorded 7 Sept. 1762

SAWYERS, William — Will Book 2, Page 85

Inventory and appraisal of the estate of William Sawyers made by John Ballard, Bennett Holloway and Spettle Pully - value 14 pounds - returned to Court by Grace Sawyers, administratrix.

Recorded 1 Sept. 1761

WILLS, John (Wells ?) — Will Book 2, Page 86

An account current of the estate of John Wills - 1757-1760 - returned to Court by William Lucas, admin.

Account approved by John Speed and Henry Delony, Comm. 18 March 1760.

Recorded 6 May 1760

GORDON, Gilbert — Will Book 2, Page 87

Inventory and appraisal of the estate of Gilbert Gordon deceased, made 12 Feb. 1762 by Isaac Holmes, Samuel Holmes, Jr., and Wm (illegible) - value 23 pounds 14 shillings 7 pence returned to Court.

Recorded 2 March 1762

BUGG, Sherwood — Will Book 2, Page 88

The account current of the estate of Sherwood Bugg, Sr. deceased, returned to Court by John Bugg, admin.

Account approved 1 June 1762 by John Speed and Henry Delony, Comm.

Recorded 1 June 1762

WILBORN, John — Will Book 2, Page 88

Account current of the estate of John Wilborn, deceased returned to Court by William Harris, Exec.

Account approved 2 March 1762 by Rich[d] Witton and W. Goode, Comm.

Recorded 3 March 1762

HIDE, Thomas — Will Book 2, Page 90

Inventory and appraisal of the estate of Thomas Hide, deceased, made 27 May 1762 by Jacob Royster, William Colbreath and Owen Franklin - no total value given.

Recorded 1 June 1762

HOLLOWAY, George — Will Book 2, page 91

An account current of the estate of George Holloway, deceased, returned to Court 5 Dec. 1760 by Henry Delony executor.

Balance due orphans of George Holloway, deceased, 247 pounds 1 shilling 2 pence - account approved 5 May 1761 by John Speed and Tho[s] Lanier, Comm.

Recorded 5 May 1761

WELLS, George — Will Book 2, Page 92

Inventory and appraisal of the estate of George Wells, deceased, made by Geo. Walton, John Hailey, Tho[s] Nance and John Wills - value 288 pounds 12 shillings.

Recorded 4 May 1762

COLBREATH, John — Will Book 2, Page 94

A further inventory of the estate of John Colbreath, deceased, returned to Court by Daniel McNeil, Exec.

Recorded 4 Nov. 1760

NORVELL, Hugh — Will Book 2, Page 94

Inventory and appraisal of the estate of Hugh Norvell, deceased, made by Stephen Mallet, William Ballard and Daniel Gorre - value 106 pounds - returned to Court.

Recorded 2 Sept. 1760

SAUNDERS, Francis — Will Book 2, Page 96

By order of the December Court 1760, we, John Coe, William Hamp and John Cox, Junr., have appraised the estate of Francis Saunders, deceased, on 6 Dec. 1760 - value 61 pounds 9 shillings 3 pence.

Recorded 3 July 1761

SEAT, Josiah — Will Book 2, Page 97

An inventory and appraisal of the estate of Josiah Seat deceased, pursuant to order of Lunenburg County Court dated in December 1761, made 30 January 1762 by John Bressie, John Jones and George More returned to Court - no value given.

Recorded 2 March 1762

RUTHERFORD, James — Will Book 2, Page 99

Settlement of the administration of William Rutherford on the estate of James Rutherford, deceased, approved 7 Aug. 1760 by James Hunt and Wm Caldwell, Comm.

Recorded 4 Nov. 1760

WILLIS, Edward — Will Book 2, Page 100

By order of the November Court 1761, we, John Flyn, Wm Hunt and John Ragsdale, have appraised the personal estate of Edwd Willis, deceased, as was delivered to us - value 272 pounds 11 shillings.

Recorded 7 Sept. 1762

SMITH, Zachariah — Will Book 2, Page 102

Inventory and appraisal of the estate of Zachariah Smith, deceased, made 1 June 1761 by Thomas Anderson, Jacob Royster and John Jones - value 378 pounds 5 shillings 9 pence - returned to Court.

Recorded 7 July 1761

EDMUNDSON, Thomas — Will Book 2, Page 103

Inventory and appraisal of the estate of Thomas Edmundson, deceased, made 1 Sept. 1760 by Isaac Holmes, John Hern and Peter Parrish - value 44 pounds 8 shillings 7½ pence - returned to Court by Randle Bracey, exec.

Recorded 3 Sept. 1760

GREEN, Henry — Will Book 2, Page 106

Inventory and appraisal of the estate of Henry Green in accordance with the order of May Court 1761 made 29 July 1761 by George Moore, Daniel Gold and Peter Overby - no value given.

Recorded 4 Aug. 1761

YANCEY, John — Will Book 2, Page 107

Inventory and appraisal of the estate of John Yancey, deceased, in accordance with the order of Court May 1761, made 1 June 1761 by Jacob Royster, Owen Franklin and Edmund Colbreath - no value given - returned to Court.

Recorded 2 June 1761

HOLLOWAY, George — Will Book 2, Page 108

An inventory of the estate of George Holloway, deceased made 20 September 1759 by John Ballard, Dennis Larke and Geo. Baskervill - value 163 pounds 8 shillings - ordered recorded.

Recorded 3 June 1760

DOBBYNS, William — Will Book 2, Page 110

An account of Joseph Williams, Gent., of the estate of William Dobbyns, deceased, approved by Clement Read and Jas Taylor, Comm., 22 August 1761.

Recorded 2 Nov. 1761

HOBSON, Nicholas — Will Book 2, Page 118

Inventory and appraisal of the estate of Nich Hobson, deceased, of Lunenburg County, taken 24 December 1759 by William Wilson, Jeremiah Hatcher and William McDow, returned to Court by Agnes Hobson, Edward Goode and John Hobson. Value 315 pounds 1 shilling.

Recorded 6 May 1760

HUGHEY, Humphrey (Huey) — Will Book 2, Page 119

Inventory and appraisal of the estate of Humphrey Hughey by order of Court dated 25 July 1760, made by Joshua Mabry, Amos Tims, Senr. and Hutchins Burton 1 Sept. 1760 - value 54 pounds 8 shillings 6 pence - returned to Court.

Recorded 2 Sept. 1760

DRUMRIGHT, James — Will Book 2, Page 120

An account current of the estate of James Drumright, deceased, (including the expense of going to Goochland on said estate) returned by James Williams, admin.

Account examined 10 Nov. 1760 by John Speed and Henry Delony, Gents, and approved.

Recorded 2 Dec. 1760

BAILEY, Henry — Will Book 2, Page 122

Inventory and appraisal of the estate of Henry Bailey

made in accordance with order of Court 5 May 1761 by Thomas Járod, Stephen Mize and Jeremiah Mize returned to Court.

Recorded 5 Aug. 1761

RUTHERFORD, James — Will Book 2, Page 125

An account of sales of the estate of James Rutherford, deceased - total 126 pounds 11 shillings 11 3/4 pence - returned to Court and ordered recorded.

Recorded 4 Nov. 1760

FUQUA, William — Will Book 2, Page 129

Memorandum of the appraisement of the estate of William Fuqua, deceased, in Bedford County, made by Michael Prewit, Joseph Williams and Thomas Greenwood 1 October 1761, returned to Court by John and Joseph Fuqua, executors.

Recorded 6 Oct. 1761

In obedience to the written order directed to us before Nat Terry (Justice), we have appraised five head of cattle to be of the value of 4 pounds 7 shillings 6 pence - 18 Sept. 1761. /s/ Wm Robson, Thos Robertson and John Dun. Memorandum of appraisal returned to Court by John Fuqua and Joseph Fuqua, executors.
Halifax County

Recorded 6 Oct. 1761

WARD, Richard — Will Book 2, Page 131

Pursuant to an order of the Court in Lunenburg County held February 1762, we, Jones Raynald, Joel Walker, and Warren Walker, have appraised the estate offered us by Perrin Alday, executor of the estate of Richard Ward, deceased, in Cumberland County, which is valued in Current Money as follows - 73 pounds 18 shillings 8 pence. /s/ Fryday 30th April 1762.

Recorded 4 May 1762

BACON, John — Will Book 2, Page 132

An account of the estate of John Bacon, deceased, according to the appraisement returned to us by Mr. Lyddal Bacon.

Division of Slaves

Legatees:

Nathaniel Bacon	William Journey
Edmond Bacon	Sarah Bacon
William Bacon	Susannah Bacon
Francis Estes	Mary Bacon

Division made 4 January 1760 by Mat Marable and John Speed.

Settlement of the estate of John Bacon, deceased, heirs William Bacon, Nath[l] Bacon, Edmond Bacon, Francis Estes, Elizabeth Journey, wife of Will[m] Journey, Sarah Bacon, Sus[h] Bacon and Mary Bacon each paid 60 pounds. Returned by Matthew Marable and John Speed, Gent, Commissioners.

Recorded 7 May 1760

JAMES, John — Will Book 2, Page 134

An account current of the estate of John James, deceased, returned by Jno. Jeffries, administrator, ordered recorded.

Recorded 3 Sept. 1761

CHILES, Henry — Will Book 2, Page 135

Inventory and appraisal of the estate of Henry Chiles, deceased, made 15 July 1756 by John Williams, Ja[s] Daws and John Regsdale - value 256 pounds 13 shillings 3 pence ordered recorded.

Recorded 6 May 1760

CALDWELL, William — Will Book 2, Page 137

According to an order of Court to us directed, we have appraised the estate of William Caldwell, deceased, Friday, May y[e] 8th 1761 - value 175 pounds 18 shillings 9 pence. /s/ James Cunningham, Francis Winn, John East

Recorded 7 July 1761

LIDDERDALE, William — Will Book 2, Page 140

Pursaant to the order of the Lunenburg County Court of June 1759, we, John Flyn and Thomas Wiles, have appraised the estate of William Lidderdale - value 108 pounds 7 shillings 2 pence.

Recorded 7 Sept. 1762

WARD, Richard — Will Book 2, Page 143

Pursuant to an order of the Court held in Lunenburg County February 1762, we, Sam[l] Johnston, Sam[l] Davis and Rob[t] Woods, have appraised the estate offered to us by Perrin Alday, executor of the estate of Richard Ward, deceased, which in current money is as follows - 518 pounds 2 shillings 6 pence.

Recorded 4 May 1762

WHEELER, Mary — Will Book 2, Page 144

Inventory and appraisal of the estate of Mary Wheeler,

deceased, made by John Buzbee, Nathaniel Robinson and William Stroud pursuant to an order of the Lunenburg Court, returned by Edmond Taylor, administrator.

Sale of the estate of Mary Wheeler made 16 Feb. 1760 - total 15 pounds 5 shillings 11½ pence.

Recorded 1 July 1760

MEDLEY, Isaac — Will Book 2, Page 146

NAMES: Wife - mentioned in will but not by name
Son - Joseph Medley - bequest of half of the tract of land I now live on.
Son - James Medley - bequest of other half of said tract of land after his mother's death.
Daughter - Frances Medley - furniture
Daughter - Lucy Medley - furniture
Son - Isaac Medley - rifle gun
Remainder of household goods, money, debts and other property to wife for widowhood to raise and maintain the children.
Sons to be of age at nineteen years.
At death of my wife, property to be sold and divided among my children.

Executors: Benjamin Bridgforth, Peter Cole and Drury Moore.
Witnesses: Daniel McKee, Benjamin Eddins and Drury Moore
Will dated 13 July 1760 — Recorded 7 Sept. 1762

Note: Executors named refused to qualify, and Matthew Turner qualified as administrator with the will annexed with James Blackwell and William Ussery as his securities.

NICHOLS, William — Will Book 2, Page 147

NAMES: Wife - Mary Nichols
Son - William Nichols
Daughter - Eleanor Hughit (Hewit ?)
Bequests - To wife one-third of all movable estate.
To son all land and two-thirds of remaining movable estate.
To daughter the other one-third.

Executors: John Orr, Junr. and William Nichols, Junr.
Witnesses: George Scott, John Orr, Robert Neally
Will dated 31 Dec. 1762 — Recorded 10 Feb. 1763

McCLENAHAN, James — Will Book 2, Page 148

Inventory and appraisal of the estate of James McClenahan, deceased, made by Robert Montgomery, Patt Sharkey and James Montgomery January ye 10th 1763 - value 22 pounds 10 shillings - returned to Court by William Snodgrass.

Recorded 10 Feb. 1763

DUDGEON, John — Will Book 2, Page 149

Inventory and appraisal of the estate of John Dudgeon, deceased, made by David Caldwell and Jo^s Mitchell - no value given.

Recorded 10 March 1763

ADKINS, John (Cornwall Parish) — Will Book 2, Page 152

NAMES: Wife - mentioned in will but not by name
Bequest to wife of one-third of all movable property and place where I now live for life.
Son - Francis Adkins - 150 acres where he now lives adjoining Alexander McKie, Samuel Johnston and others.
Son - Edward Adkins - 100 acres where I now live at his mother's death.
Daughter - Agnes Adkins
Daughter - Rachel Adkins
Bequeathed to two daughters two-thirds of all stock and household goods.
Son - William Adkins - 1 shilling Sterling
Son - John Adkins - 1 shilling Sterling
Daughter - Mary Creighton - 1 shilling Sterling
Son - Benjamin Adkins - 1 shilling Sterling

Executors: Son Francis Adkins and James Taylor
Witnesses: David Maddox, Wilson Maddox, Michal Maddox
Will dated 10 April 1762 — Recorded 10 March 1763

BRESSIE, Francis — Will Book 2, Page 153

By virtue of the annext order of the Court of Lunenburg County, we William Cocke, Benjamin Pulliam and George Bruce, being first sworn, have proceeded to appraise the estate of Francis Braisey (sic), deceased as follows: - No total given. Returned to Court by Eliza Bressie.

Recorded 10 March 1763

DUDGEON, John — Will Book 2, Page 155

A true account of the sales of the estate of John Dudgeon, deceased, - no total given - returned to Court by John McNeese.

Recorded 10 March 1763

LOGAN, David — Will Book 2, Page 157

NAMES: Wife - not named in will and evidently deceased
Son - John Logan
Second son - David Logan - bequest 300 acres of land on Wolleges (Wallace ?) Creek adjoining Revd W. Henry and John Logan - he paying my daughter Jean Logan (when she is of age) 25 pounds Virginia money.

Son by law - George Moore - 200 acres of land in Halifax at the falls of Elkhorn - he to pay to my daughter Jean 5 pounds when she be of age.

Son-in-law - Angus Campbell - 265 acres of land in Halifax above George Moore on Elkhorn Creek.

My 800 acres at the head branches of Walloses Creek to be sold and money equally divided among my children, viz:

John Logan, Eliza Moore, David Logan, Mary Caldwell, Martha Campbell and Jean Logan.

I give to my son John Logan my Great Bible.

Personal property divided between daughter Jean Logan and son David Logan.

Executors: John Logan and Robert Caldwell
Witnesses: John Caldwell, Jr., Wm Leaton, Richard Dougan and Dudley Rutledge

Will dated 17 March 1763 — Recorded 14 April 1763

PALMER, Richard — Will Book 2, Page 159

Pursuant to an order of the Court of Lunenburg County, we, the subscribers, have divided the slaves of the estate of Rich Palmer, deceased, the other part of the personal estate being sold, and the accounts for settling and dividing the same not yet being rendered to us for a division.

Division of Slaves

Lot 1 -	To Mary Palmer	Lot 4 -	To John Palmer
Lot 2 -	Eliza Palmer	Lot 5 -	Peter Atkins *
Lot 3 -	Edward Palmer	Lot 6 -	William Palmer

* Who married Grissell Palmer

Division as made by Edmund Taylor, John Camp and Thos Anderson

Recorded 14 April 1763

NICHOLS, William — Will Book 2, Page 160

Inventory and appraisal of the estate of William Nichols, deceased, of Lunenburg County, made by Thos Price

Geo. Cardwell and Daniel Slaydon 18 March 1763 - value 35 pounds 8 shillings 10½ pence.

Recorded 14 April 1763

Will Book 2, Page 162

Sales of the personal estate of William Nichols, deceased, made 18 March 1763 - value 44 pounds 12 shillings 2 pence - returned to Court and ordered recorded.

Recorded 14 April 1763

PATTERSON, Irvin — Will Book 2, Page 163

Inventory and appraisal of the estate of Irvin Patterson, deceased, of Lunenburg County, made by John Caldwell, Andrew Rodgers and William Hardwitch - value 151 pounds 13 shillings 7 pence - returned to Court and ordered recorded.

Recorded 12 May 1763

GRYMES, Francis — Will Book 2, Page 165

An account current of the estate of Francis Grymes, deceased, returned to Court by John and William Lawson, executors - approved by James Hunt and James McCraw, Commissioners.

Recorded 12 May 1763

MEALER, Nicholas — Will Book 2, Page 166

St. James Parish, Lunenburg County

NAMES: Wife - Ann Mealer
Bequest to wife of a negro man and all of personal estate during widowhood.
Son - Peter Nealer
Bequest of 100 acres of land at upper end of land I now live on and stock.
Son - Matthias Mealer
Bequest of remainder of tract of land I now live on. Matthias not to possess the land until death or marriage of his mother.
Daughter - Mary Mealer to have my house for a home as long as she is single.
Daughter - Elizabeth Bullington - one shilling.
Daughter - Ann Whittle (Whitlow ?) - one shilling.
Son - Nicholas Mealer - to be given a slave when he is of age 21 years.

After death or marriage of my wife, all of my personal estate to be sold and divided among my children, namely: William Mealer, James

Mealer, Thomas Mealer, Mary Mealer, Sarah Mealer and Judith Mealer.
The tract of land on Little Bluestone Creek that I bought of Thomas Tate (may be sold back to him) but if he does not take it my executors are to sell the land and put to money to such use as they may think proper.

I desire that the 200 acres of land (I own) in Henrico County be sold by Mr. William Gathright and title made to purchaser by my executors.

I appoint Thom[s] Anderson guardian to my (minor) children with right to bind them out them to learn a trade if he thinks proper.

Executors: Friend Thomas Anderson and son Matthias Mealer.
Witnesses: William Mealer, Mary (M) Mealer and Eliz (X) Cox.

Will dated 21 Aug. 1762 — Recorded 12 May 1763

Note: Thomas Anderson qualified as executor with Rich[d] Mullins and William Mealer as his securities.

COCKERHAM, Henry — Will Book 2, Page 168

Settlement of the estate of Henry Cockerham, deceased, and an account of the sales of sundry goods by Jn[o] Hix made 8 May 1761. Approved by Lyddal Bacon and Thomas Tabb, Comm. No legatees listed.

Recorded 9 June 1763

BARTLEY, James — Will Book 2, Page 170

We, the appraisers John Callaham, Drewry Hawkins and Drewry Moore, being first sworn before W Goode one of his Majesties Justice of the Peace for the said County, have appraised the estate of James Bartley, deceased, in current money. (No total given)

Recorded 14 July 1763

ROBERSON, Abraham (Robertson) — Will Book 2, Page 172

We, John Wilson, Bruce Miller and John Buzbee, being appointed and sworn, have appraised the estate of Abraham Roberson this 14 May 1763. Returned to Court by Mary Buzbee, admn[x], but no total stated.

Recorded 14 July 1763

CUNNINGHAM, James — Will Book 2, Page 172

Inventory and appraisal of the estate of James Cunningham made 1 December 1762 by Thomas Pettus and Joseph Davis returned to Court and ordered recorded. Total value not stated.

Recorded 14 July 1763

GORDON, John * Will Book 2, Page 176

An account current of the estate of John Gordon, deceased, returned to Court by Thos. Lett, Administrator - and approved by Henry Delony and Benjn Baird, Comm.
Recorded 11 Aug. 1763

* This is also mentioned as the estate of Gilbert Gordon indicating that the full name may have been John Gilbert Gordon.

WATSON, John Will Book 2, Page 176

NAMES: Wife - mentioned in will but not by name.
Son - William Watson - bequest of the plantation whereon he now lives and other land.
Son - John Watson - all of my wearing apparrel except my great coat.
Son-in-law - William Poole - a feather bed and furniture.
Son - Burwell Watson - horse, bridle and saddle and my great coat.
After payment of debts, all of the rest of my estate to go to my wife during her life or widowhood, but after either, I desire that my land be sold and money arising from the sale to be divided among my sons - Henry Watson, Burwell Watson, Isaac Watson and Jacob Watson. They to pay to my son James Watson the sum of 5 pounds.
Executors: My wife (not named) and son Henry Watson
Witnesses: John Lett Cook, Reuben Cook, James Lett and Reuben Vaughan.
Will dated 6 March 1763 Recorded 11 Aug. 1763

Will Book 2, Page 178

The Just and True Inventory of the Goods and Chattels of the estate of John Watson, deceased, returned to Court and ordered recorded - no total given.
Recorded 8 Sept. 1763

GLENN, Tyree Will Book 2, Page 179

NAMES: Wife - Mary Glenn
Son - Jeremiah Glenn - all land I hold upon Reedy Creek, six negroes, etc.
If Jeremiah dies without lawful heirs, all to revert to my estate and be equally divided among the person hereafter named.
Son - John Glenn - all that tract of land I purchased of David Lyle on the Meherrin River and a survey of land I bought of Drury

Allen on the branches of Kitts Creek
Son - William Glenn - all that tract of land whereon at present I live, containing by estimation 216 acres, and a survey of land I bought of the late Abraham Cocke.
Remainder of my estate consisting of a tract of land lying on Twitty's Creek, negroes, stock, etc. to remain undivided until my son John reaches age 21. Then it shall be divided equally among my spouse Mary and my sons John and William and my daughters Anne and Sarah Glenn.

I order and appoint that my spouse Mary shall have bed, board and all accomodations suitable to her station, such as she has enjoyed since becoming my lawful wife, during the remainder of her life.

Executor: Son Jeremiah Glenn
Witnesses: David Hopkins, Henry Blagrave and John Cook
Will dated 2 July 1763 — Recorded 8 Sept. 1763

WRENN, Thomas — Will Book 2, Page 181

An account current of the estate of Thomas Wrenn, deceased, May 1762 to August 1763 - returned to Court by James French, administrator - approved 30 August 1763 by James Taylor and Thom[s] Bedford, Comm.

Recorded 8 Sept. 1763

CERTAIN, Thomas, Senr. — Will Book 2, Page 182

In obedience to an order of the Court, we John Fuqua, Joseph Bayse and W[m] Cunningham, the subscribers, have appraised the estate of Thomas Certain, Senr., deceased brought before us, to-wit: 16 pounds 10 shillings 6 pence.

Additional estate of Thomas Certain, Senr., appraised 7 October 1763 - value 14 pounds 17 shillings - returned to Court by William Mayes, administrator.

Recorded 13 Oct. 1763

CAMPBELL, Matthew — Will Book 2, Page 184

NAMES: Wife - not named in will and evidently deceased
Son - Hohn Campbell - gives a horse
Daughter - Salle Campbell - gives a cow

I ordain that my land and dwelling place be sold, and all of my stock and movable property (except that given above) be sold, and moneys to be equally divided among my respective children when they arrive of age.

Executors: W[m] Rutherford, John Holt and Peter Rawlins
Witnesses: W[m] Rutherford, Peter Rawlins, John Holt and Peter MacCown

Will dated 13 Sept. 1763 — Recorded 13 Oct. 1763

FOSTER, John, Junr — Will Book 2, Page 185

Inventory and appraisal of the estate of John Foster, Junr., deceased, made by Willm Watkins, Thos Spencer, Henry Isbell and C. Read - no total given - returned to Court and ordered recorded.

Recorded 13 Oct. 1763

An account and settlement of the estate of John Foster, Junr., deceased, approved 12 Oct. 1763 by C. Read and Thom^{s} Spencer, Comm.

Recorded 13 Oct. 1763

HENDERSON, Joseph — Will Book 2, Page 189

NAMES: Wife - Esther Henderson

I desire that my lands, stock and other property remain unsold for the support, raising and schooling of my children, viz: Mary Henderson, James Henderson, Robert Henderson, John Henderson, Joseph Henderson, Samuel Henderson and Abraham Henderson.

I appoint friends James Boyd and Abraham Erwin to be trustées and have oversight of my wife and children.

If my wife remarries, my trustees to sell all mòvable property and give to my wife one-third. The rest to be divided among my children as they come of age. As they come to a suitable age, my children may be bound out to trades.

Executor: Wife Esther Henderson
Witnesses: Robt Erwin and Martha Boyd
Will dated 25 March 1763 — Recorded 10 Nov. 1763

Notation on page 191 that will of Anthony Hughes is recorded on page 302 which ought to be recorded here.

HUGHES, Anthony — Will Book 2, Page 191

NAMES: Wife - Elizabeth Hughes

Bequest of entire estate to wife Elizabeth Hùghes for her natural life, and at her death divided as stated hereunder.

Granddaughter - Sarah Hughes Chamberlin
Daughter - Mary Chamberlin
Son-in-law - William Chamberlin
Grandchildren - Thomas Chamberlin, William Chamberlin, Elizabeth Felps (Phelps ?) Susannah Chamberlin and Sarah Hughes Chamberlin

At death of my wife, I give my granddaughter

Sarah Hughes Chamberlin my land and plantation, slave named Moll, saddle and riding horse.

Gives daughter Mary Chamberlin slave for life and 50 acres of land and house she now lives in, and at her death to Sarah Hughes Chamberlin.

Rest of my estate to be divided among my grandchildren named above.

Executor: Wife Elizabeth Hughes.

Witnesses: Christopher Hudson, Antony Kitchen and Mary Kitchen

Will dated 24 April 1760 Recorded 10 Nov. 1763

BARTLEY, James Will Book 2, Page 191

An account of the settlement of the estate of James Bartley, deceased, returned by Jane Bartley, admin[x]. Examined and approved by Mat Marable and Benj[n] Whitehead.

Recorded 8 Dec. 1763

GLENN, Tyree Will Book 2, Page 193

Pursuant to an order of Court bearing date of 8 September last, we Henry Blagrave, David Hopkins and John Scott, the subscribers, have this day - 10 October 1763 - met and appraised the estate of Mr. Tyree Glenn, deceased, as follows: 1382 pounds 2 shillings.

Recorded 9 Feb. 1764

CAMPBELL, Matthew Will Book 2, Page 195

Pursuant to an order of Court, we William Price, John White and Matt[w] Watson, your commissioners, have appraised the estate of Matthew Campbell as - 76 pounds 10 shillings 9 pence.

Recorded 9 Feb. 1764

KEY, William Will Book 2, Page 197

An inventory and appraisal of the estate of the Rev. Mr. William Key, Clerke - value 103 pounds 8 shillings 9 pence.

Will Book 2, Page 203

A further inventory of the estate of Rev. Mr. Key - value 157 pounds 19 shillins 3 pence - returned by us, Peter Fontaine and Clem[t] Read, admins.

Recorded 9 Feb. 1764

Note: Page 205 is blank.

KEY, William Will Book 2, Page 206

An account of sales of the estate of the Rev[d] William

Key, deceased, returned to Court by Peter Fontaine and Clem^t Read - total 138 pounds 14 shillings 3 pence.

Recorded 9 Feb. 1764

CAMPBELL, Matthew — Will Book 2, Page 210

An account of sales of the estate of Matthew Campbell, deceased, made 19 October 1763 - total 183 pounds 13 shillings 5 pence. Lists foodstuff for support of his children.

Recorded 9 Feb. 1764

EMBRY, William — Will Book 2, Page 213

Mem^o of sundries of the estate of Mr. William Embry, deceased, which are divided agreeable to his will by David Garland and John Ragsdale, executors 22 Nov. 1763 Value 823 pounds 5 shillings 3 pence.

We the subscribers having met in order to divide the personal estate of William Embry and finding the same already done by the executors, and Tscharner Degraffenreidt and Elizabeth his wife, who was the widow of the said William Embry, and all parties agreeing, we make this report, 16 December 1763, finding each part to be 137 pounds 4 shillings.
/s/ Wm Gordon, Richd Williams, Matt Burt

Recorded 14 April 1764

MEDLEY, Isaac — Will Book 2, Page 214

An inventory of the appraisement and sale of the estate of Isaac Medley, deceased. The whole sail (sic) amounted to 32 pounds 17 shillings 1 pence - returned to Court by Matthew Turner, administrator.

Recorded 12 April 1764

COMER, John — Will Book 2, Page 215

A division of the estate of John Comer, deceased, between Annis Sammons, widow of the deceased, William Comer, Elizabeth Lucas, Daniel Comer, Samuel Comer and Annis Comer, made 9 December 1762 by your Commissioners Sherwood Walton, John Cox, Charles Sullivant and Valentine Brown.

Heirs of the Deceased

William and Annis Sammons
William Comer, son of the deceased
John and Elizabeth Lucas, daughter of the deceased
Daniel Comer, son of the deceased
Samuel Comer, son of the deceased
Annis Comer, daughter of the deceased

Report of the division of the estate of John Comer, deceased, dated 11 December 1762.

Recorded 12 April 1764

LUNDERMAN, Abraham — Will Book 2, Page 216

(Cornwall Parish, Lunenburg County)

NAMES: Wife - Jane Lunderman
Bequest of land and plantation "where I now live", all movable property and all money to hèr and her heirs forever.
Executors: Wife Jane, Joel Townes and David Gwinn
Witnesses: John Cook, Matthew Roberson and Nancy Roberson
Will dated 1 Feb. 1764 — Recorded 12 April 1764

DUDGEON, John — Will Book 2, Page 217

An account current of the estate of John Dudgeon, deceased, returned by John McNeese, admin^{r}.

Approved by P. Carrington and Ja^{s} Taylor, Comm.

Recorded 12 May 1764

HAILEY, Edward — Will Book 2, Page 222

In obedience to an order of the Lunenburg Court bearing date of 8 March 1764, we Anthony Fullilove, Robt Beasley and Frederick Nance, the sûbscribers, have appraised the estate of Edward Hailey, deceased, as 12 pounds 14 shillings 6 pence.

Recorded 14 June 1764

LUNDAY, Richard — Will Book 2, Page 223

Estate to be sold by my executors, except my black horse and wrone (sic) mare.

After payment of debts, the remainder of my estate I give to be equally divided between the children of Joseph Smith (not named) of Sussex County.

I give my wrohe mare to Anne Russell of Lunenburg County.

The black horse to remain in the family of Joseph Smith.

Executor: Merriott Bland
Witnesses: Sarah Bland and Ann Russell
Will dated _______ 1764 — Will not signed

Note: No date of qualification recorded, or date of the recording of the will given. Presumably recorded 14 June 1764.

It is assumed that the will was proven by the witnesses, and that Merriott Bland qualified as executor.

MEALER, Nicholas | Will Book 2, Page 224

We have proceeded to appraise in current money the estate of Nicholas Mealer, deceased, and do certify that the same is as followeth: 259 pounds 5 shillings 2 pence. Given under our hands this 14 June 1764. /s/ John Flyn, Dav[d] Halliburton, John Jeffries, Jr.

Recorded 14 June 1764

LUNDERMAN, Abraham | Will Book 2, Page 225

Whereas we Joel Townes, Robt Brumfield and George Gwin being by an order of Court appointed to appraise the estate of Abraham Lunderman, deceased, being first sworn before David Caldwell, one of the Justices of the county, do appraise the estate as followeth: No total given.

Recorded 12 June 1764

CUNNINGHAM, John | Will Book 2, Page 227

In obedience to an order of Court dated 12th April, we Samuel Hopkins, Edmund Bugg and Anselm Bugg, the subscribers, being first sworn, have appraised the estate of John Cunningham, deceased as follows: The whole amount is 18 pounds 9 shillings 3 pence.

Recorded 12 July 1764

CHAPMAN, Moses | Will Book 2, Page 227

By an order of the Court of Lunenburg County, we Amos Hix, Samuel Bugg and James Sandifer appraised the estate of Moses Chapman 11th July 1764 - value 21 pounds 3 pence.

Recorded 13 Sept. 1764

LUNDY, Richard | Will Book 2, Page 229

By an order of the Court, we Samuel Bugg, Amos Hix and James Sandifer, the subscribers, have appraised the estate of Richard Lundy, deceased, 11th July 1764, viz: 46 pounds 5 shillings 11 pence.

Recorded 13 Sept. 1764

LEWIS, James | Page Book 2, Page 230

NAMES: Wife - Elizabeth Lewis
I give to my wife Elizabeth Lewis four negroes, her full part of movable property and her dower part in my lands.
Daughter - Catherine Lewis - gives (at age 18) 200 pounds money, negroes and other property that my executors think convenient.
Daughter - Mary Lewis - gives (at age 18) 200 pounds money.
If either daughter dies underage, the bequests above to go to the other.

Son - James Lewis - I desire that my estate be kept together until my son James becomes age 21 years.

Whereas I sold to my brother Howel Lewis one tract of land on the north side of the Roanoke River which I purchased from John Robinson, Junr., containing about 125 acres for which I received the money but made no deed to him, I now confirm this to him.

All of the rest of my estate, both real and personal, to be divided equally among my three sons, James Lewis, John Lewis and Charles Lewis, by my executors as soon as convenient after my son James comes to age 21 years.

Executors: Wife Elizabeth Lewis, brother Howel Lewis, Robert Lewis and friends Phillip Taylor and Edmund Taylor.

Witnesses: Edmund Taylor, Robert Lewis, Jr., Ann Taylor and Charles Kennon

Will dated 5 May 1764 — Recorded 14 Sept. 1764

COX, John — Will Book 2, Page 232

(John Cox the elder, St. James Parish)

NAMES: Wife - Mary Cox
Bequest to wife of eight slaves, personal property. At her death or marriage shall be divided as my son John Cox shall see fit.
Daughter - Anne Ship - negroes
Granddaughter - Nancy Ship, daughter of Anne Ship - negro
Daughter - Delitia Chandler - slaves to be disposed of by my son John for her use
Grandchildren - Rebecca and Keziah Chandler
Daughter - Mary Smithson - negro
Granddaughter - Keziah Smithson, daughter of Mary Smithson - negro
Daughter - Edith Minor - negro
Granddaughter - Letitia Minor, daughter of Edith Minor - negro
Daughter - Tabitha Cox - negro
Son - Frederick Cox - personal property for life
Granddaughter - Frank[y] Coleman Cox, daughter of Frederick Cox
Son - Bartley Cox - land and plantation at death or marriage of my wife Mary Cox.
Granddaughter - Mary Cox, daughter of John Cox
Son - John Cox - residue of my estate

Executors: Wife Mary Cox and son John Cox

Witnesses: Benjamin Clark, William Náish, Thomas Taylor and Benjn Whitehead, Junr.

Will dated 15 July 1764 — Recorded 15 Sept, 1764

PARRISH, Charles Will Book 2, Page 235

NAMES: Wife - not named in will and evidently deceased
Son - Charles Parrish
Son - David Parrish
Son - Robert Parrish
Son - Jowell (Joel ?) Parrish
I desire that my eldest son Charles may have manor plantation and negroes
Bequests:
David Parrish - negro
Robert Parrish - negro
Jowell Parrish - negro
Daughter - Hannah Parrish - negro
Daughter - Millissie Parrish - negro
Daughter - Lucy Parrish - negro
Daughter - Mary Patillo - one shilling
I desire that my two youngest sons to have schooling out of my estate
I desire that no division of my est- be made until my son Charles comes to age 21 years

Executors: John Parrish, Charles Parrish and Millissie Parrish
Witnesses: Mathew Hubbard, John Hamack, John Gunn and Cha[s] Hamlin, Junr.
Will dated 15 Feb. 1764 Recorded 11 Oct. 1764

CERTAIN, Thomas, Senr. Will Book 2, Page 236

Inventory of all and singular the goods and chattels of Thomas Certain, Senr., late of Lunenburg County, deceased, taken and sold 19 Nov[r] 1763 by me whose name is here under written. Total 14 pounds 9 shillings 11 pence.

Another inventory of goods taken and sold 22 Oct. 1763 - value 18 pounds 8 shillings.

/s/ William Mayes, admin.
Recorded 11 Oct. 1764

CHANDLER, Joseph Will Book 2, Page 238

(St. James Parish, Lunenburg County)

NAMES: Wife - Sarah Chandler
After payment of debts, gives to wife personal property to be hers to dispose of as she wishes.
Son - William Chandler - land and plantation where he now lives.
(Son-in-law ?) - Richard Burnes - 330 acres of land where he now lives.

Son - Joel Chandler - land and plantation where I now live.

Executor: Son Joel Chandler

Witnesses: Guy Smith, Thomas Anderson and Cathren Rose

Will dated 2 March 1763 Recorded 11 Oct. 1764

ROBERSON, John (Robinson ?) Will Book 2, Page 239

NAMES: Wife - Sarah Roberson

Son - John Roberson

To wife Sarah Roberson, personal property, interest on my money until my son John comes of age.

To my son John, my money when he comes to age 21 years.

To son John 10 pounds due from James Leach to buy a horse and bridle.

Remainder of my estate, real and personal, to my wife Sarah for life and then to my son John.

Executor: Edward Lewis

Witnesses: Bazwell Wagstaff, John Maynard and Matt^w Turner

Will dated 4 Sept. 1764 Recorded 8 Nov. 1764

BACON, John Will Book 2, Page 240

An account current of the estate of John Bacon, deceased, returned by Lyddal Bacon, admin.

Approved by Mat Marable and John Speed, Comm.

Recorded 8 Nov. 1764

PALMER, Capt. Richard Will Book 2, Page 242

By an order of Court dated 14 July 1763, we have settled the estate of Capt. Richard Palmer, deceased.

A balance of 134 pounds 8 shillings 6½ pence is to be divided between the wife and five children.

/s/ Robt Munford and John Camp

Recorded 13 Dec. 1764

WARD, Richard Will Book 2, Page 243

A further inventory and appraisement of the estate of Richard Ward, deceased, made by Robt Woods, Saml Davis and Saml Johnson - value 9 pounds 5 shillings - returned to Court by Perrin Alday, exec.

Recorded 13 Dec. 1764

INGRAM, Samuel Will Book 2, Page 243

Pursuant to an order of the Lunenburg County Court, bearing date of 13 December 1764, we Christopher Billups, Roger Madison and Jacobus Christopher have appraised the estate of Samuel Ingram, deceased - value 412 pounds 18 shillings 2 pence. Returned to Court and ordered recorded.

Recorded 14 March 1765

ADKINS, John — Will Book 2, Page 245

An account of sales of the estate of John Adkins, deceased, value 74 pounds 4 shillings 2 pence, returned to Court by W. James Taylor and Francis Adkins, execs.

Pursuant to an order of Court, account settled 5 March 1765 by Clem[t] Read and Thomas Bouldin, Comm.

Recorded 14 March 1765

DYER, Robert Henry — Will Book 2, Page 246

NAMES: Wife - not named in will and deceased
Son - Robert Dyer
Daughter - Susannah Phillips - personal property
Grandson - Robert Phillips
Grandson - John Phillips

Bequest to grandson Robert Phillips one-half of land and plantation where I now live.

Bequest to grandson John Phillips the other half of the land and plantation where I now live.

Grandson - Dyer Phillips

If either Robert or John Phillips dies before age 21 or without heirs, his part to go to grandson Dyer Phillips.

Granddaughter - Mary Phillips (sister of Robert and John Phillips)- furniture.
Granddaughter - Mary Dyer
Granddaughter - Martha Dyer

Balance of estate to be sold by executors and (after payment of debts) money to be divided between Mary and Martha Dyer, daughters of son Robert Dyer, on their marriage or at lawful age. If either dies, other to have all of this bequest.

Executors: Son (in-law) George Phillips and friend Reps Jones, Senr.

Witnesses: Sam[l] Meanley, William Rhodes and James Amos

Will dated 22 Nov. 1764 — Recorded 14 March 1766

PHILLIPS, Preseller — Will Book 2, Page 248

NAMES: Son - John Phillips
Daughter - Sukey (Susanna) Barnes Phillips

Bequest to son John three negroes and my part of the estate of my mother at her death.

Bequest to daughter Susanna Barnes Phillips two negroes, furniture and other person al property to be given her at age 18.

If Susanna Barnes Phillips dies be-

fore age 18, John Phillips to have her part of my estate.
Son - Micajah Phillips - 20 shillings Sterling and no more.
Residue of my estate to go to John Phillips.
Executor: No executor named in will
Witnesses: Lod[k] Farmer, Benajah Thompson, John Moore, Junr. and Edward Shephard
Will dated 23 July 1764 — Recorded 14 March 1765

PHILLIPS, Priscilla — Will Book 2, Page 250

In obedience to an order of the Lunenburg County Court, we, John Foster, Frederick Nance and James Foster, have inventoried and appraised the estate of Priscilla Phillips, deceased. No total value given.

Recorded 11 April 1765

PARRISH, Charles — Will Book 2, Page 251

Pursuant to an order of Court dated 11 October 1764, we, Thomas Chambers, Ch Hamlin, Jr., and Reps Jones, have appraised the estate of Charles Parrish, deceased, and return this report 13 June 1765 - value 420 pounds 13 shillings 9 pence.

Recorded 13 June 1765

EASLEY, Thomas — Will Book 2, Page 253

Settlement of the estate of Thomas Easley, deceased, - value 150 pounds 5 pence - in the hands of Matt[w] Watson administrator - made by Col. Tabb and W[m] Easley of Charlotte County.
Examined by James Taylor and Elisha White, Comm.

Recorded 13 June 1765

PATTERSON, Erwin — Will Book 2, Page 254

Settlement of the estate of Erwin Patterson, deceased, by Thom[s] Rogers, executor.
Examined and approved 11 June 1765 by James McCraw, James Hunt and David Caldwell, Comm.

Recorded 13 June 1765

Will Book 2, Page 258

The settlement of the estate of Erwin Patterson deceased to 21 December 1764 with John Mills, executor, examined and approved by James McCraw, James Hunt and David Caldwell, Commissioners, 11 June 1765.

Recorded 13 June 1765

OWEN, Walter — Will Book 2, Page 260

NAMES: Wife - Joyce Owen
Son - Barnett Owen
Son - William Owen
Son - David Owen
Son - Joseph Owen

Bequest: Wife Joyce to have use and occupation of my whole estate for her natural life or widowhood.

At her death or remarriage, my son Barnett shall have all of the estate lent to my wife.

If my son Barnett dies without lawful issue, then my estate is to be equally divided between my three sons William, David and Joseph Owen.

Executor: Son Barnett Owen
Witnesses: Lyddal Bacon and Young Stokes
Will dated 27 January 1765 — Recorded 11 July 1765

EDMUNDSON, Thomas — Will Book 2, Page 261

An account current of the estate of Thos Edmundson, deceased, - April 1764-August 1765 - returned by Randall Bracey, examined and approved by John Speed and Henry Delony, Comm.

Recorded 8 Aug. 1765

DYER, Robert Henry — Will Book 2, Page 263

Inventory and appraisal of the estate of Mr. Robert Henry Dyer made 3 April 1765 by Chas Hamlin, Jr., Robt Chappell and John Hammock - value 54 pounds 5 shillings 11 pence - returned to Court.

Recorded 8 April 1765

FIRTH, Daniel — Will Book 2, Page 265

An account current of the estate of Daniel Firth, deceased, approved by Clemt Read and Paul Carrington, Com.

Recorded 9 Aug. 1765

CUNNINGHAM, James — Will Book 2, Page 267

Inventory and appraisal of the estate of James Cunningham, deceased, made March ye 19th 1765 by David Hopkins Robert Bailey and Henry Crenshaw - no total given - returned to Court and ordered recorded.

Recorded 12 Sept. 1765

OWEN, Walter — Will Book 2, Page 271

A true and perfect inventory and appraisement of the

estate of Walter Owen, deceased, made by Joseph Minor, Jo[s] Billups and Jacobus Christopher - value 28 pounds 7 pence - returned to Court and ordered recorded.

Recorded 12 Sept. 1765

JOHNSON, Joseph — Will Book 2, Page 273

An account current of the estate of Joseph Johnson, deceased, returned to Court by Sherwood Walton, exec.
Examined and approved by Lyddal Bacon, Henry Blagrave and Jonathon Patterson, Jr., Comm.

Recorded 10 Oct. 1765

READ, Clement — Will Book 2, Page 278

Inventory and appraisement of the estate of Clem[t] Read, deceased, taken by Jno White, Elisha White and Jno Holt this 4th June 1764 - value 3803 pounds 17 shillings 9½ pence - returned to Court

Recorded 10 Oct. 1765

Will Book 2, Page 285

Mr. Isaac Read in account with Clemt Read, eldest son and heir of Clemt Read, deceased, signed in full for his share of his father's slaves - value 297 pounds 19 shillings 7 pence. 23 October 1764.

Page 285

Miss Nancy Read in account with Clemt Read eldest son and heir of Clemt Read, deceased, receipt for her share of her father's slaves signed by Clemt Read her guardian. 23 October 1764. 297-19-7.

Page 286

Mrs. Mary Read in account with Clem[t] Read eldest son and heir of Clem[t] Read, Deceased, for her third of the negroes - value 951 pounds - belonging to the estate of her late husband Clem[t] Read, deceased.

Page 287

Mr. Thomas Nash in account with Clem[t] Read eldest son and heir of Clem[t] Read, deceased, receipt for the share of the orphans of Mary Nash of the slaves of Clem[t] Read - value 297 pounds 19 shillings 7 pence.

Page 287

Received 23 October 1764 of Clem[t] Read the sum of 65 pounds 9 shillings 7 pence current money for Clemt Nash and Mary Owen Nash, orphans of Mary Nash, deceased daughter of Clem[t] Read, deceased. /s/ Mary Read

Mr. Paul Carrington in account with Clement Read, eldest son and heir of Clemt Read, deceased, by his wife's share of slaves belonging to Clemt Read, deceased - 297 pounds 19 shillings 7 pence.

Receipt from Paul Carrington for his wife, Margaret Carrington, for her share of slaves belonging to her father Clemt Read, deceased. 23 October 1764.

Page 289

Mr. Thomas Read in account with Clemt Read, eldest son and heir of Clemt Read, deceased - 297 pounds 19 shillings 7 pence.

Receipt from Thomas Read for his full share of the slaves of the estate of his father, Clemt Read, dec'd.

Page 290

Mr. Edmund Read in account with Clemt Read, eldest son and heir of Clemt Read, deceased - 297 pounds 19 shillings 7 pence.

Receipt of Mary Read guardian of Edmund Read.

Page 290

Mr. Jonathon Read in account with Clemt Read, eldest son and heir of Clemt Read, deceased - 297 pounds 19 shillings 7 pence.

Receipt of Mary Read guardian for Jonathon Read.

Page 291

Mr. Clemt Read, eldest son and heir at law of Clemt Read, deceased, to the widow and orphans of Clemt Read.

The whole amount of negroes		2867-0-0
To what Paul Carrington received in Clement Read's lifetime		240-0-0
To what Thomas Nash received in Clement Read's lifetime		232-10-0
		3339-10-0
Mary Read's third	955-13-4	
Paul Carrington his 8th	297-19-7	
Clemt Read his 8th	297-19-7	
Orphans of Thomas Nash - 8th	297-19-7	
Thomas Read his 8th	297-19-7	
Isaac Read his 8th	297-19-7	
Edmund Read his 8th	297-19-7	
Jonathon Read his 8th	297-19-7	
Nancy Read her 8th	297-19-7	3339-10-0

Settled this 3rd day Octo 1765, as witness our hands - /s/ Clemt Read, Mary Read, Thoms Read, Is Read P. Carrington

CUNNINGHAM, James | Will Book 2, Page 292

An account of the sales of the estate of James Cunningham held the 21st day of March 1765 - no total given

Recorded 12 June 1766

WELLS, George | Will Book 2, Page 297

An account current of the estate of George Wells, deceased - 1759-1766 - approved by Christr Billups and Jos. Williams, Comm.

Recorded 12 June 1766

Will Book 2, Page 298

Notation in margin of page

At a Court held 10 Nov. 1768, it appears an article was omitted from the inventory of the estate of George Wells, deceased.

Ordered that credit for a negro fellow named Harry - value 65 pounds be given.

/s/ Wm Taylor Cl.C.

LEWIS, James | Will Book 2, Page 299

Pursuant to an order of the Lunenburg Court, we Samuel Hopkins, Anselm Bugg and William Davis, the subscribers being first sworn, have proceeded to appraise the estate of James Lewis, deceased as follows: value 1641 pounds 14 shillings.

The above is all of the estate belonging to Capt. James Lewis, deceased, that was shown us by the executors as certified under our hands this 15th day of October 1765.

Recorded 10 July 1766

PARKER, William, Senr | Will Book 2, Page 304

An account of sales of the estate of William Parker, Senr., made 15 November 1765 - total 29 pounds 19 shillings 4½ pence.

Recorded 11 Dec. 1766

ROBERTSON, John | Will Book 2, Page 306

We John Potter, Bazell Wagstaff and John Maynard, the subscribers, being first sworn before Col. Munford one of the Justices of the Peace of Lunenburg County, have appraised the estate of John Robertson, deceased - valued at 24 pounds 9 shillings 9 pence on 23 Feb. 1765

Recorded 10 July 1766

ANNOTATION

WILLIAMS, Benjamin

John Robertson made oath according to law and obtained certificate of administration on the estate of Benjamin Williams, deceased, whereupon he with William Howard, Gent. his security acknowledged bond.
July Court 1746 Order Book 1, Page 28

SANFORD, Robert

Ann Sanford is granted letters of administration on the estate of her late husband Robert Sanford, deceased, and with Seth Pettypool and Francis Ray her securities entered into and acknowledged bond.
December Court 1746 Order Book 1, Page 80

SANFORD, Robert, Junr.

Ordered that the Church Wardens of Cumberland Parish in this County do bind out Robert Sanford, orphan of Robert Sanford, deceased, according to law.
March Court 1747 Order Book 1, Page 396

SANFORD, Ann

John Forrest and Ann his wife, late widow and administratrix of Robert Sanford, deceased, failing to give Seth Pettypool and Francis Ray security pursuant to order of this Court,

It is ordered that John Forrest and wife Ann do deliver up the said estate to Pettypool and Ray (who were securities for Ann) to be disposed of by them in such manner as they think best for their indemnity.
May Court 1747 Order Book 1, Page 189

SANFORD, John

John Pettypool is appointed guardian of John Sanford, orphan of Robert Sanford, deceased, and with Seth Pettypool his security acknowledged bond.
November Court 1747 Order Book 1, Page 297

RAILEY, Robert

Ordered that the Church Wardens of Cumberland Parish do bind out Robert Railey, orphan of Mary Railey.
September Court 1747 Order Book 1, Page 262

CLEMENTS, John

Thomas King having heretofore been appointed guardian for John Clements, orphan of John Clements, deceased, with

William Howard his security acknowledged bond as the law directs.
September Court 1747 Order Book 1, Page 263

HUNT, William

Letters of administration granted to William Mobberly on the estate of William Hunt, deceased, who with Matthew Talbot his security acknowledged bond for that purpose.
March Court 1747/48 Order Book 1, Page 389

Ordered that William Verdeman, John Price, Rice Price and John Mead, or any three of them, do appraise the personal estate of William Hunt, deceased.
March Court 1747/48 Order Book 1, Page 390

VALRAVEN, Cornelius

Letters of administration granted to William Embry on the estate of Cornelius Valraven, deceased, who with James Meredith his security acknowledged their bond.
April Court 1748 Order Book 1, Page 405

Ordered that Edward Nix, Valentine Nix, William Mayes and Peter Willson, or any three of them, do appraise the personal estate of Cornelius Valraven.
April Court 1748 Order Book 1, Page 406

YOUNG, John

Elizabeth Young is granted administration on the estate of her late husband, John Young, deceased, who with Matthew Talbot her security entered into bond.
June Court 1748 Order Book 2, Page 12

Ordered that Thomas Bouldin, Abraham Martin, David Gwin and Joseph Perrin, or any three of them, do appraise the slaves, if any, and the personal estate of John Young, dec.
June Court 1748 Order Book 2, Page 12

YOUNG, Philip

Philip Young, orphan of John Young. deceased, being of lawful age for that purpose, came into Court and made choice of his sister Elizabeth Young to be his guardian, who with Thomas Jones and John Gwin her securities acknowledged bond for that purpose.
July Court 1748 Order Book 2, Page 37

JAMES, Thomas

Francis James is granted administration on the estate of Thomas James, deceased, and with Thomas Worthy his security acknowledged bond.
October Court 1748 Order Book 2, Page 77

CANNADY, Andrew

On the Motion of Elizabeth Cannady she is granted administration on the estate of Andrew Cannady, deceased, and with John Logan her security acknowledged their bond.
October Court 1748 — Order Book 2, Page 77

EVANS, John

Ordered that the Church Wardens of Cumberland Parish in this County do bind out Rebecca Evans, orphan of John Evans, deceased.
February Court 1748/49 — Order Book 2, Page 106

Ordered that the Church Wardens of Cumberland Parish do bind out Margaret Evans, orphan of John Evans, deceased, to John Middleton.
February Court 1748/49 — Order Book 2, Page 116

CANNADY, David

David Logan is appointed guardian to David Cannady, orphan of Andrew Cannady, deceased, and he is to appear at the next to give security.
February Court 1748/49 — Order Book 2, Page 116

STOVALL, Hannah

On the Motion of Tandy Walker for administration on the estate of Hannah Stovall, deceased, It is ordered that a summons issue to George Stovall of Albemarle County commanding him to appear at the next Court to show his objection thereto, if any he hath.
July Court 1749 — Order Book 2, Page 186

Tandy Walker is appointed administratror of the estate of Hannah Stovall, and with Silvanus Walker his security gave bond for the administration on said estate.
October Court 1749 — Order Book 2, Page 211

CANNADY, John

Ordered that the Church Wardens of Cumberland Parish do bind out John Cannady and Elizabeth Cannaday, orphans of Andrew Cannady, deceased, according to law.
October Court 1749 — Order Book 2, Page 219

EVANS, John

Ordered that the Church Wardens of Cumberland Parish do bind out Amos Evans, orphan of John Evans, deceased, according to law.
October Court 1749 — Order Book 2, Page 219

STEVENS, James

Ordered that the Church Wardens of Cumberland Parish do bind out Richard Stevens, orphan of James Stevens, deceased, according to law.
January Court 1749/50 Order Book 2, Page 265

TUTER, Patrick (Tudor ?)

Richard Brown is granted letters of administration on the estate of Patrick Tuter, deceased, and with James Burton his security acknowledged their bond for that purpose.
January Court 1749/50 Order Book 2, Page 252

Ordered that William Irby, John Hannah, John Nichols and John LeGrand, or any three of them, do appraise the slaves and personal estate of Patrick Tuter, deceased.
January Court 1749/50 Order Book 2, Page 252

WILLY, John

Sarah Willie, orphan of John Willy, deceased, came into Court, and being of lawful age for that purpose, made choice of Thomas Blanks to be her guardian he to give bond, whereupon he with William Caldwell his security entered into and acknowledged bond.
July Court 1750 Order Book 2, Page 288

SMITH, William Thornton

The petition of Ann Smith, administratrix of William Thornton Smith, deceased, against John Goode for debt is ordered dismissed.
October Court 1750 Order Book 2, Page 367

SMITH, Henry

Mary Smith is granted letters of administration on the estate of Henry Smith, deceased, and with William Hill, Gent and Jeremiah Claunch her securities acknowledged her bond.
April Court 1751 Order Book 2, Page 388

Ordered that Thomas Lanier, Matthew White, James Coleman and Caleb Blackwelder, or any three of them, do appraise the estate of Henry Smith, deceased.
April Court 1751 Order Book 2, Page 388

DALTON, William

Ordered that the Church Wardens of Cumberland Parish do bind out John Dalton, orphan of William Dalton, deceased, according to law.
April Court 1751 Order Book 2, Page 391

CHANDLER, William

Ordered that the Church Wardens of Cumberland Parish do bind out William Chandler, son of William Chandler, deceased according to law to Benjamin Dixon son of Thomas Dixon.
June Court 1748 Order Book 2, Page 11

Ordered that the Church Wardens of Cumberland Parish do bind out Abraham Chandler, son of William Chandler, to Matthew Talbot, Gent.
July Court 1750 Order Book 2, Page 298

COLE, William

Ordered that the Church Wardens of Cumberland Parish do bind out Thomas Cole, orphan of William Cole, deceased, according to law to John Baird.
February Court 1748/49 Order Book 2, Page 103

USSERY, John

Sarah Ussery, widow of John Ussery, deceased, summoned to appear at the next Court to show cause why she has not administered on the estate of her deceased husband.
October Court 1750 Order Book 2, Page 348

William Ussery granted administration on the estate of John Ussery, deceased, and with John Tabor and John Blackwell, his securities, entered into and acknowledged bond.
October Court 1751 Order Book 2, Page 461

Ordered that John Williams, Reps Jones, William Rivers and Robert Moore, or any three of them, do appraise the personal estate of John Ussery, deceased.
October Court 1751 Order Book 2, Page 467

MURPHY, Mary

Mary Murphy, being of lawful age for that purpose, came into Court and made choice of Joseph Echols to be her guardian. He to appear at the next Court to give bond.
August Court 1748 Order Book 2, Page 73

JETER, Joseph

Ordered that Young Stokes, Richard Stokes, John Wynne and Thomas Wynne, or any three of them, do appraise the personal estate of Joseph Jeter, deceased.
February Court 1748/49 Order Book 2, Page 108

LAURENCE, Benjamin

Letters of administration is granted John Lawson on the

estate of Benjamin Laurence, deceased, and with William Lawson his security entered into and acknowledged bond.
April Court 1751 | Order Book 2, Page 398

HOWARD, Dianna

Dianna Howard, executrix of her husband Francis Howard, has since intermarried with George Farrar.
January Court 1751/52 | Order Book 2, Page 251

Elizabeth Howard, orphan of Francis Howard, being of legal age (to choose her own guardian), came into Court and made choice of George Farrar to be her guardian.

Elinor Howard, orphan of Francis Howard, she not being of lawful age (to choose her own guardian), George Farrar is appointed guardian to said orphan.
June Court 1752 | Order Book 2½-A, Page 58

BARRY, John

On the Motion of Catherine Barry, who made oath as the law directs, certificate for letters of administration is granted her on the estate of John Barry, deceased, who with Hugh Lawson, Gent. her security acknowledged bond.
October Court 1751 | Order Book 2, Page 447

GWIN, John

Elizabeth Gwin, relict of John Gwin, deceased, voluntarily came into Court and relinquished her administration on the estate of her deceased husband to Thomas Bouldin, who with John Twitty and John Cox his securities acknowledged bond.
April Court 1752 | Order Book 2½-A, Page 18

Note: See will of David Gwin who mentions son John Gwin apparently deceased.

William Jones (who intermarried with Elizabeth relict of John Gwin deceased) is appointed guardian to John Gwin (an infant under the age of 21 years heir at law of the said John Gwin deceased) to defend a caveat entered by Peter Fontaine, Junr., against the said infant and others (on the part of the said infant) for 800 acres of land lying and being in the County of Halifax on the south fork of Terable (sic) Creek.
May Court 1754 | Order Book 3, Page 9

David Gwin, orphan of David Gwin, deceased, came into Court, and being of lawful age for that purpose, made choice of Thomas Bouldin, Gent., to be his guardian
December Court 1755 | Order Book 4, Page 61

A receipt from David Gwin to Thomas Bouldin is exhibited in Court, and on the Motion of said Thomas Bouldin is ordered to be recorded.
July Court 1757 Order Book 4, Page 312

JONES, Thomas

Thomas Jones and Dorothy Jones, orphans of Thomas Jones deceased, came into Court, and being of lawful age for that purpose, made choice of Godfrey Jones to be their guardian.
September Court 1752 Order Book 2½-A, Page 249

A receipt from Thomas Jones and Dorothy Gwin to Godfrey Jones is exhibited in Court by the said Godfrey Jones, guardian of the said Thomas and Dorothy and is ordered to be recorded.
November Court 1760 Order Book 6, Page 188

M.B. ___ June 1757 - David Gwin and Dorothy Jones
Ref: Lunenburg County Marriage Records - 1746-1761

JERRARD, Joseph

Ordered that Mary Jerrard, relict of Joseph Jerrard, be summoned to appear at the next Court to show cause why she has not administered on the estate of her said husband.
May Court 1752 Order Book 2½-A, Page 38

Mary Jerrard came into Court and voluntarily relinguished administration of her husband's estate to any person the Court thought fit to administer it, and the Court doth appoint Hampton Wade as administrator, who with Joseph Williams his security acknowledged bond.
Order Book 2½-A, Page 38

NOBLES, Robert

Ordered that the Church Wardens of Cumberland Parish do bind out Robert Nobles, orphan of Robert Nobles, deceased, according to law to Francis Ray.
June Court 1752 Order Book 2½-A, page 49

SATTERWHITE, Thomas

Michael Satterwhite came into Court and made choice of his father, Thomas Satterwhite, to be his guardian, who with Francis Bracey his security acknowledged his bond.
June Court 1752 Order Book 2½-A, Page 57

DABBS, Joseph

Anthony Hoggate is appointed guardian to William Dabbs, orphan of Joseph Dabbs, deceased, and gave bond with James Hunt his security.

June Court 1752 Order Book $2\frac{1}{2}$-A, Page 63

CAMPBELL, Walter

Tabitha Campbell, administratrix (with the will annexed) of the estate of Walter Campbell, deceased, sues for debt.

July Court 1752 Order Book $2\frac{1}{2}$-A, Page 118

UNDERWOOD, Thomas

The petition of Elizabeth Underwood, administratrix of Thomas Underwood, deceased, against Glidewell Orrell - rec.

September Court 1752 Order Book $2\frac{1}{2}$-A, Page 253

BAKER, William

Zachariah Baker is appointed guardian of James Baker, orphan of William Baker, deceased, who with Francis Bracey and James Coleman his security acknowledged bond.

Judith Baker, William Baker and Sarah Baker, orphans of William Baker, came into Court, and being of lawful age for that purpose, made choice of Zachariah Baker to be their guardian.

October Court 1752 Order Book $2\frac{1}{2}$-A, Page 292

JACKSON, Mary

Mary Jackson, an orphan of lawful age, came into Court and made choice of Henry Jackson to be her guardian, and he with John Speed and Dennis Lark his securities gave bond.

November Court 1753 Order Book $2\frac{1}{2}$-A, Page 312

Henry Jackson, Guardian of Mary Jackson, orphan of John Jackson, deceased, returned an account to Court which is ordered to be recorded.

October Court 1756 Order Book 4, Page 186

HUNT, John

Ordered that the Church Wardens of Cumberland Parish do bind out John Hunt, orphan of John Hunt, deceased, according to law.

November Court 1752 Order Book $2\frac{1}{2}$-A, Page 391

JOLLY, Henry

Ordered that the Church Wardens of Cumberland Parish do bind out Henry Jolly, orphan of Henry Jolly, deceased according to law.

February Court 1753/54 Order Book $2\frac{1}{2}$-A, Page 453

FRANCIS, John

Micajah Francis is granted letters of administration on the estate of John Francis, deceased, and gave bond with James Brumfield his security.
February Court 1753/54 Order Book 2½-A, Page 456

CRISWELL, Uriah (Cliswell)

James Criswell, orphan of Uriah Criswell, deceased, came into Court, and being of lawful age for that purpose, made choice of William Saffold to be his guardian, who is accordingly appointed and with Jeffery Russell his security acknowledged their bond.
February Court 1753/54 Order Book 2½-A, Page 459

CARGILL, John

Nathaniel Harrison, administrator de bonis non by Elizabeth Cargill, administratrix of John Cargill, deceased against Edward Peters, recorded.
February Court 1753/54 Order Book 2½-A, Page 508

COBB, Winfield

Ordered that the Church Wardens of Cumberland Parish do bind out William Cobb and Hannah Cobb, orphans of Winfield Cobb according to law.
April Court 1753 Order Book 2½-A, Page 585

DALTON, William

Ordered that the Church Wardens of Cumberland Parish do bind out William Dalton and Ann Dalton, orphans of William Dalton.
April Court 1753 Order Book 2½-B, Page 26

WALKER, Judy *

Ordered that the Church Wardens of Cumberland Parish do bind out Silvanus Walker, Tandy Walker, William Walker, Joel Walker, Langford Walker, Ann Walker and Elizabeth Walker according to law.
September Court 1753 Order Book 2½-B, Page 370

* See will of Juday (Judith) Walker.

BAKER, Samuel

Bartholomew Baker, orphan of Samuel Baker, being of legal age for that purpose, came into Court and made choice of Mark Thornton to be his guardian who gave bond with Thomas Willingham his security.
September Court 1753 Order Book 2½-B, Page 438

LESTER, George

Ordered that the Church Wardens of Cumberland Parish do bind out Edward Lester, George Lester and Jeremiah Lester to Thomas Farrar according to law.
February Court 1754 Order Book 2½-B, Page 532

RAWLINS, John

On the Motion of Henry May the Court do appoint him, the said Henry May, guardian of William Rawlins, orphan of John Rawlins, whereon he with Thomas Jones his security entered into a bond for that purpose.
September Court 1754 Order Book 3, Page 189

SHORTER, John

Ordered that the Sheriff of this County summon Kindness Shorter, relict of John Shorter, deceased, to appear at the next Court to show cause why she doth not administer on her said husband's estate.
October Court 1754 Order Book 2½-B, Page 194

Ordered that the Church Wardens of Cornwall Parish do bind out James Shorter, orphan of John Shorter, deceased, according to law.
July Court 1758 Order Book 5, Page 110

WRIGHT, John

On the Motion of John Speed for letters of administration on the estate of John Wright, deceased, ordered that Amey Wright, widow of John Wright, do appear at the next Court to show cause why she does not administer on the said estate. John Speed is to take into his possession said estate and take care of same.
May Court 1755 Order Book 3, Page 339

Laban Wright, orphan of John Wright, deceased, came into Court, and being of lawful age for that purpose, made choice of John Speed to be his guardian, who with Henry Delony, John Ballard and George Baskervill entered into and acknowledged bond.
May Court 1755 Order Book 3, Page 339

ROYALL, Joseph

John Humphries exhibited and made oath to an account against the estate of Joseph Royall, deceased, for two pounds which is ordered to be certified.
May Court 1755 Order Book 3, Page 341

TWITTY, John *

John Ruffin, Gent., Complainant against John Twitty, Defendant - The defendant having departed this life since the last continuance, the suit aforesaid abates (because of death).
June Court 1755 — Order Book 3, Page 376

* Inventory and appraisal of the estate of John Twitty returned to Court 5 July 1755.

SMITH, John

Elizabeth Smith, orphan of John Smith, deceased, being of lawful age for that purpose, came into Court and made choice of John Smith, her brother, to be her guardian, who with James Hunt, Gent., his security, acknowledged bond.
October Court 1755 Order Book 4, Page 3

BROOKS, Richard

Susannah Brooks is granted administration on the estate of Richard Brooks, deceased, her late husband, and with David Gentry and Robert Brooks her securities, acknowledged bond.
December Court 1755 Order Book 4, Page 64

Ordered that John Williams, Reps Jones, Samuel Gentry and Drury Moore, or any three of them, do appraise the slaves and personal estate of Richard Brooks, deceased.
December Court 1755 Order Book 4, Page 64

EAST, Thomas

Thomas East, orphan of Thomas East, deceased, came into Court (and being of lawful age for that purpose),made choice of John East to be his guardian, who with James East and William Robertson his securities acknowledged bond.
February Court 1756 Order Book 4, Page 76

DALTON, John

Ordered that John Dalton, orphan of William Dalton, be removed from Henry Bolton, to whom he is now bound, and be bound out by the Church Wardens to Silvanus Stokes, son of Young Stokes.
February Court 1756 Order Book 4, Page 110

YOUNG, Martha

Martha Young, orphan of John Young, deceased, came into Court (she being of lawful age for that purpose) made choice of Pinkithman Hawkins to be her guardian who with George Walton and Henry Howard his securities acknowledged bond.
July Court 1756 Order Book 4, Page 157

DABBS, William

William Dabbs, orphan of Joseph Dabbs, deceased, came into Court (and being of lawful age for that purpose) made choice of Daniel Hankins to be his guardian who gave bond.
July Court 1756 Order Book 4, Page 158

SAWYER, Elizabeth

On the Motion of Thomas Stevens (who made oath according to law) certificate for obtaining letters of administration of the estate of Elizabeth Sawyer, deceased, is granted him on his giving security. Whereupon he together with Thomas Satterwhite his security entered into and acknowledged their bond for the due administration of said estate.
July Court 1756 Order Book 4, Page 167

Ordered that George Farrar, Isaac Mitchell, Jacob Mitchell and John Johnson, or any three of them, do appraise in current money the slaves and personal estate of Elizabeth Sawyer, deceased.
July Court 1756 Order Book 4, Page 167

FRANCIS, Thomas

James Arnold, guardian of Ann Francis orphan of Thomas Francis, deceased, exhibited and made oath to an account of the said orphan's estate, which is ordered to be recorded.
August Court 1756 Order Book 4, Page 169

Ann Francis, orphan of Thomas Francis, deceased, came into Court, and being of lawful age for that purpose, made choice of James Arnold to be her guardian who is accordingly appointed he giving security, Whereupon he together with Henry Delony entered into and acknowledged bond for that purpose.
August Court 1755 Order Book 3, Page 402

Received of Mr. James Arnold the whole estate that Mr. Thos Francis, Father to my wife Ann, left her, Viz^t. Four Slaves. /s/ George Ingram
November Court 1756 Order Book 4, Page 513

SAWYER, Tabitha

Ordered that the Church Wardens of Cumberland Parish do bind out Tabitha Sawyer, orphan of Elizabeth Sawyer, deceased, to Nicholas Rober(t)son according to law.
September Court 1756 Order Book 4, Page 204

POOL, Thomas

Thomas Anderson is granted administration on the estate of Thomas Pool, deceased, who with Thomas Hawkins his secur-

ity acknowledged bond for that purpose.
March Court 1757 — Order Book 4, Page 265

DAVIS, John

William Davis is granted administration on the estate of John Davis, deceased, who together with Edward Davis his security entered into and acknowledged bond.
March Court 1757 — Order Book 4, Page 267

Lucy Davis, orphan of John Davis, deceased, came into Court, and being of lawful age for that purpose, made choice of William Davis to be her guardian who with James Cocke his security entered into and acknowledged bond.
March Court 1757 — Order Book 4, Page 267

John Davis, orphan of John Davis, deceased, came into Court, and being of lawful age for that purpose, made choice of William Davis to be his guardian, who with Thomas Hawkins his security acknowledged bond.
June Court 1757 — Order Book 4, Page 299

Baxter Davis, orphan of John Davis, deceased, came into Court, and being of lawful age for that purpose, made choice of William Davis to be his guardian.
June Court 1757 — Order Book 4, Page 299

BRYAN, Jemima

Ordered that the Church Wardens of Cumberland Parish do bind out James Bryan, orphan of Jemima Bryan, to Charles Hunt according to law.
March Court 1757 — Order Book 4, Page 268

POOL, Robert

William Pool is granted administration on the estate of Robert Pool, deceased, who with Adam Pool his security entered into and acknowledged their bond.
March Court 1757 — Order Book 4, Page 268

Ordered that Clack Courtney, Samuel Man(n)ing, Thomas Taylor and Wade Ward, or any three of them, do appraise the estate of Robert Pool, deceased.
March Court 1757 — Order Book 4, Page 296

YOUNG, Anne

Anne Young, orphan of John Young, deceased, came into Court, and being of lawful age for that purpose, made choice of (Thomas) Norrel (Norvell) to be her guardian who with Pinkethman Hawkins his security acknowledged bond.
April Court 1757 — Order Book 4, Page 278

PERKINSON, Francis

Ordered that the Church Wardens of Cumberland Parish do bind out Mary Perkinson, orphan of Francis Perkinson, deceased to John Logan according to law.
May Court 1757 Order Book 4, Page 290

JONES, Robert

On the Motion of William Jones he is appointed guardian to Leanner Jones, orphan of Robert Jones, deceased, who with David Garland and William Ballard his securities entered into bond for that purpose.
May Court 1757 Order Book 4, Page 297

MADISON, Henry

Isbell Madison, orphan of Henry Madison, deceased, came into Court (being of lawful age for that purpose) made choice of Tscharner DeGraffenreidt to be her guardian who with George Walton his security acknowledged bond.
August Court 1757 Order Book 4, Page 335

Henry Madison, orphan of Henry Madison, deceased, came into Court, and being of lawful age for that purpose, made choice of Roger Madison to be his guardian who with George Crimes (Crymes) and Daniel Claiborne his securities entered into bond for that purpose.
August Court 1757 Order Book 4, page 335

MATTHEWS, John

John Matthews, son of Mary Matthews, came into Court, and being of lawful age for that purpose, made choice of his mother to be his guardian.
June Court 1756 Order Book 4, page 129

Petition of John Twitty Matthews, by Mary Matthews his guardian and next friend, against John Robertson .. ordered recorded.
October Court 1757 Order Book 4, Page 405

ALLEN, Jeremiah

Ordered that the Church Wardens of Cornwall Parish do bind out Charles Allen, orphan of Jeremiah Allen, deceased, according to law to John Hight, and the Court do adjudge the said orphan to be twelve years of age.
December Court 1757 Order Book 5, Page 24

WILBORN, John

Ordered that the Church Wardens of Cumberland Parish do bind out Thomas Wilborn, orphan of John Wilborn, deceased,

to John Childers according to law.
September Court 1758 — Order Book 5, Page 111

CALDWELL, Henry

Ordered that the Church Wardens of Cornwall Parish do bind out Henry Caldwell, orphan of William Caldwell to John Caldwell.
December Court 1757 — Order Book 5, Page 23

COMER, John

Ordered that the Church Wardens of Cumberland Parish do bind out William Comer, orphan of John Comer, deceased, to Joseph Ship.
December Court 1757 — Order Book 5, Page 27

Peter Farrar is appointed guardian for James Powell Cocke, Chastain Cocke and Stephen Cocke, orphans of James Cocke, deceased, he giving bond according to law.
November Court 1758 — Order Book 5, Page 117

DODD, David

Ordered that the Church Wardens of Cumberland Parish do bind out David Dodd, Agnes Dodd, William Dodd and John Dodd, orphans of David Dodd and Agnes Dodd, deceased, according to law.
December Court 1758 — Order Book 5, Page 122

ELLIS, Elizabeth

Ordered that the Church Wardens of Cumberland Parish do bind out Sarah Ellis, daughter of Elizabeth Ellis, deceased, to Lewis Dupree according to law.
May Court 1759 — Order Book 5, Page 142

PREWIT, Daniel

Ordered that the Church Wardens of Cornwall Parish do bind out Lucy Prewit, daughter of Daniel Prewit, deceased, to Henry Austin according to law.
May Court 1759 — Order Book 5, Page 142

WILLIS, John

Ordered that the Church Wardens of Cumberland Parish do bind out Samuel Willis, orphan of John Willis, deceased according to law.
May Court 1758 — Order Book 5, Page 76

FLIPPEN, Thomas

Ordered that the Church Wardens of Cornwall Parish do

bind out Thomas Flippen, orphan of Thomas Flippen, deceased, to Thomas Bedford according to law.
May Court 1758 Order Book 5, Page 76

GARROTT, Joseph

Ordered that the Church Wardens of Cumberland Parish do bind out James Garrott, orphan of Joseph Garrott, according to law.
May Court 1759 Order Book 5, Page 142

Ordered that the Church Wardens of Cumberland Parish do bind out William Garrott, orphan of Joseph Garrott, according to law.
May Court 1759 Order Book 5, Page 142

FRANCIS, Nathaniel

Ordered that the Church Wardens of Cornwall Parish do bind out Nathaniel Francis, orphan of John Francis, to Daniel May according to law.
May Court 1759 Order Book 5, Page 139

JONES, Martha

Martha Jones came into Court, and being of lawful age for such purpose, made choice of William Holt to be her guardian, and he to give security at the next Court for this County.
May Court 1759 Order Book 5, Page 139

MATTHEWS, William

Ordered that the Church Wardens of Cornwall Parish do bind out William Matthews, orphan of William Matthews, deceased, to Owen Sullivant according to law.
April Court 1759 Order Book 5, Page 142

LESTER, Moses

Ordered that the Church Wardens of Cornwall Parish do bind out Moses Lester, orphan of George Lester, deceased, to Henry Hudson according to law.
December Court 1757 Order Book 5, Page 23

PEARSON, Charles

Joseph Pearson, orphan of Charles Pearson, deceased, came into Court, and being of lawful age for that purpose, made choice of George Walton to be his guardian, who with Henry Isbell his security entered into and acknowledged his bond.
November Court 1758 Order Book 5, Page 116

NEAL, George

Ordered that the Church Wardens of Cumberland Parish do bind out Jonathon Neal, orphan of George Neal, deceased, to John Farrar according to law.
April Court 1758 Order Book 5, Page 65

FERRILL, Benjamin

Ordered that the Church Wardens of Cumberland Parish do bind out Benjamin Ferrell, orphan of Hubbard Ferrill, deceased, to William Ferrill according to law.
March Court 1758 Order Book 5, Page 39

WILLIAMSON, Thomas

Ordered that the Church Wardens of Cornwall Parish do bind out Elizabeth Williamson, daughter of Thomas Williamson deceased, to Paul Carrington according to law.
June Court 1758 Order Book 5, Page 87

WELLS, John

On the Motion of William Lucas, who made oath according to law, letters of administration is granted to him for probate on the estate of John Walls, deceased, whereupon he with John Speed, Gent., his security, acknowledged bond for administration on said estate.
September Court 1758 Order Book 5, Page 112

TOWNS, John

Joel Towns, guardian of Mariann Towns, orphan of John Towns, deceased, rendered an account to Court for the said orphans estate which is ordered to be recorded.
August Court 1759 Order Book 6, Page 16

FRANCIS, Lucius

Ordered that the Church Wardens of Cornwall Parish do bind out Lucius Francis, orphan of John Francis, deceased, to Henry May according to law.
August Court 1759 Order Book 6, Page 18

BILBO, Peter

Peter Bilbo, orphan of John Peter Bilbo, deceased, came into Court, and being of lawful age for that purpose, made choice of James Bilbo to be his guardian, he giving security is hereby appointed, whereupon he with Joseph Freeman his security acknowledged bond according to law.
August Court 1759 Order Book 6, Page 18

BRADLEY, William

Ordered that the Church Wardens of Cumberland Parish do bind out James Bradley, orphan of William Bradley, deceased, according to law.
November Court 1759 Order Book 6, Page 40

BACON, John

On the Motion of Lydall Bacon, Gent., who made oath according to law, certificate is granted him to obtain letters of administration (with the will annexed) on the estate of John Bacon, deceased, he giving security, whereupon he with John Cox and William Pool his securities acknowledged bond for that purpose.
December Court 1759 Order Book 6, Page 45

Sarah Bacon, orphan of John Bacon, being of lawful age for that purpose, came into Court and made choice of John Speed, Gent., to be her guardian.

John Speed, Gent., is appointed guardian for Susannah Bacon and Mary Bacon, orphans of John Bacon, deceased, who are under lawful age for that purpose, he giving security, whereupon he with David Garland his security entered into and acknowledged their bond.
December Court 1759 Order Book 6, Page 46

Note: At the same Court, Edmund Bacon made choice of John Bacon for his guardian, and Elizabeth Bacon chose Nathaniel Bacon as her guardian.

WHEELER, Samuel

Edmund Taylor is appointed guardian for William Holloway Wheeler, orphan of Samuel Wheeler, deceased, and with Pinkethman Hawkins his security acknowledged bond for that purpose.
February Court 1760 Order Book 6, Page 52

Ordered that the Church Wardens of Cumberland Parish do bind out Anne Wheeler, orphan of Samuel Wheeler, to John Bacon according to law.
June Court 1759 Order Book 6, Page 2

DRUMRIGHT, James

James Williams is appointed guardian to William Drumright, orphan of James Drumright, deceased, and with John Jennings his security entered into and acknowledged bond.
November Court 1759 Order Book 6, page 42

WHARTON, Michael

Ordered that the Church Wardens of Cornwall Parish do

bind out Samuel Wharton, orphan of Michael Wharton, to Samuel Perrin according to law.
March Court 1760 Order Book 6, Page 76

SMITH, John

Ordered that the Church Wardens of Cornwall Parish do bind out Elizabeth Smith, Judith Smith, John Smith and Phebe Smith, children of John Smith, deceased, according to law.
August Court 1760 Order Book 6, Page 155

Ordered that the Church Wardens of Cornwall Parish do bind out Ellinor Smith, daughter of John Smith, according to law.
August Court 1760 Order Book 6, Page 155

TOWNS, Caleb

Ordered that the Church Wardens of Cornwall Parish do bind out Caleb Towns, orphan of John Towns, deceased, according to law.
March Court 1761 Order Book 6, Page 223

SMITH, Charles

Drury Smith is appointed guardian for Samuel Smith and Margaret Smith, orphans of Charles Smith, deceased, and with Robert Munford his security entered into and acknowledged bond for that purpose.
March Court 1761 Order Book 6, Page 223

JOHNSON, Joseph

Joseph Williams, Gent., is appointed guardian for Elizabeth Johnson and Sisley Johnson, orphans of Joseph Johnson, deceased, and with Henry Isbell his security entered into and acknowledged bond for that purpose.
April Court 1761 Order Book 6, Page 260

BLANKS, Hannah

Marriage contract between Cornelius Cargill and Hannah Blanks, widow of Joseph Blanks.
20 March 1753 Deed Book 3, Page 293

M.B. 3 April 1753 - Cornelius Cargill and Hannah Blanks
Ref: Lunenburg County Marriage Records - 1746-1761

TWITTY, William

Deed - William Twitty, son and heir of John Twitty, to Nicholas Hobson, son of Nicholas Hobson, deceased.
21 November 1758 Deed Book 5, Page 371

BILBO, Elizabeth

Elizabeth Bilbo, widow of John Peter Bilbo, married (2) before 8 Nov. 1752 Adam Winders. (See page 35)

HAWKINS, Mary

Mary Hawkins, widow of Thomas Hawkins, married (2) before 1 Nov. 1759 John Potter.

M.B. 29 Jan. 1753 - Thomas Hawkins and Mary Howard

M.B. 16 Oct. 1759 - John Potter and Mary Hawkins
Ref: Lunenburg County Marriage Records - 1746-1761
Ref: Mecklenburg County Deed Book 1, page 81

HOWARD, Dianna

Dianna Howard, widow of Francis Howard, married (2) before 1 Jan. 1751/52 George Farrar. (See pages 9 and 131)

EMBRY, Elizabeth

Elizabeth Embry, widow of William Embry, married (2) Tscharner DeGraffendeidt.

M.B. 10 Feb. 1760 - Tscharner Degraffenreid and Elizabeth Embry
Ref: Lunenburg County Marriage Records - 1746-1761

LIDDERDALE, Sarah

Sarah Lidderdale was, apparently, the (2) wife of William Lidderdale for he seems to have married (1) Jane Clemons (Clements) widow of John Clemons.

Will (of John Clemons) brought into Court by Jane, widow of John Clemons, who since his death has married William Lidderdale.
Ref: Brunswick County Will Book 2, page 36

COMER, Annis

Annis Comer, widow of John Comer, married (2) before 9 December 1762 William Sammons. (See page 114)

SANFORD, Ann

Ann Sanford, widow of Robert Sanford, married (2) John Forrest before 1 May 1747. (See page 126)

GWIN, Elizabeth

Elizabeth Gwin, widow of John Gwin, married (2) William

Jones who, at the May Court 1754, was appointed guardian for John Gwin, Junr. heir at law of John Gwin, deceased. (See page 131)

SOME EARLY LUNENBURG COUNTY MARRIAGE RECORDS

M.B. 11 Oct. 1750 - Joseph Minor and Edith Cox

M.B. 25 April 1750 - William Holt and Rachel Jones

M.B. 5 April 1751 - Tyree Glenn and Mary Roe

M.B. 24 Oct. 1751 - Cornelius Cargill and Judith Walker

M.B. 10 Feb. 1752 - John Middleton and Martha Warkup

M.B. 11 May 1753 - James McMachen and Rebecca Cunningham

M.B. 3 July 1753 - Elijah Wells and Pheby Nance

M.B. 5 July 1753 - Robert Wooding and Mary Marable

M.B. 11 Feb. 1754 - Robert Henry and Jane Caldwell

M.B. 25 Sept. 1755 - Paul Carrington and Margaret Read

M.B. 15 May 1756 - John Satterwhite and Frances Cockerham

M.B. 22 July 1756 - Henry Blagrave and Elizabeth Stokes

M.B. 27 July 1756 - Richard Wilkins and Rebecca Twitty

M.B. 8 Feb. 1757 - Charles Allen and Betty Firth

M.B. 22 Dec. 1757 - Clement Read, Jr. and Mary Nash

M.B. 26 May 1760 - Major Weatherford and Mary Edwards
Ref: Lunenburg County Marriage Records - 1746-1761

Note: The surname AVERETT is recorded variously in early records in Lunenburg County as "Avreth", "Avorit" and "Avory".

Other variations in recording early names are found as follows: Arnold-Arnoll, Bressie-Bracey, Cannady-Kennedy, Barry-Berry, Daughtery-Daurity-Doughorty, Ealidge-Ellidge, Drumright-Drumwright, Flinn-Flyn, Fifer-Phifer, Hewit-Hughit Garrard-Jerrard, Huey-Hughey, Pool-Poole, Parsons-Persons, Prewit-Pruit, Sawyer-Sawyers, Tait-Tate, Townes-Towns, Wells-Wills, Wilborn-Wilburn, Willy-Willie, Stevens-Stephens Wilds-Wiles-Wyles and Wray-Ray.

EARLY WILLS

NAME INDEX

CPSIA information can be obtained
at www.ICGtesting.com
Printed in the USA
FFHW02n0911101018
48682259-52690FF